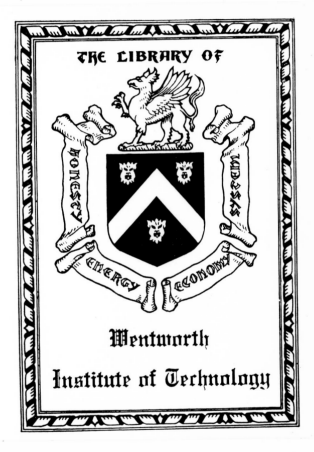

Louis L'Amour

Revised Edition

Twayne's United States Authors Series

Warren French, Editor

University College of Swansea, Wales

TUSAS 491

Louis L'Amour

Revised Edition

Robert L. Gale

University of Pittsburgh

Twayne Publishers • New York
Maxwell Macmillan Canada • Toronto
Maxwell Macmillan International • New York Oxford Singapore Sydney

Louis L'Amour, Revised Edition
Robert L. Gale

Twayne Publishers
Macmillan Publishing Company
866 Third Avenue
New York, New York 10022

Maxwell Macmillan Canada Inc.
1200 Eglinton Avenue East
Suite 200
Don Mills, Ontario M3C 3N1

Macmillan Publishing Company is part of the Maxwell Communications Group of Companies.

10 9 8 7 6 5 4 3 2 1

The paper used in this publication meets the minimum requirements of American National Standard for Information Sciences—Permanence of Paper for Printed Library Materials, ANSI Z39.48-1984. ∞™

Printed and bound in the United States of America.

Library of Congress Cataloging-in-Publication Data
Gale, Robert L., 1919–
    Louis L'Amour / Robert L. Gale. — Rev. ed.
        p.   cm. — (Twayne's United States authors series : TUSAS 491)
    Includes bibliographical references and index.
    ISBN 0-8057-7649-4 (alk. paper)
    1. L'Amour, Louis, 1908–   — Criticism and interpretation.
    2. Western stories — History and criticism.   3. West (U.S.) in
    literature.   I. Title.   II. Series.
    PS3523.A446Z67   1992
    813'.52 — dc20   91-43405
                                                                      CIP

To the memory of my parents
Erie Lee Gale (1885–1979)
Miriam Fisher Gale (1887–1984)

Contents

Preface

Louis L'Amour, a nonsmoker, died in Los Angeles of lung cancer on 10 June 1988, at the age of 80. His millions of fans were stunned. They had expected him to stay well and energetic, continue to travel and lecture, pursue his special brand of research on the Far West, Western Europe, the Middle East, and Malaysia, and write more books until the age of 95 at least.

Hints had led his readers to expect 20 or so additional novels dealing with his Sackett, Chantry, and Talon families, a volume or two continuing the adventures of the hero of *The Walking Drum,* a sequel to *Last of the Breed,* a Cheyenne trilogy, more frontier fiction (including a novel tentatively entitled *South Pass*), a novel about Louis Riel and another about H. H. Sibley, an encyclopedia about western facts and rumors and trivia, an autobiography, and possibly a "new-frontier" novel about space pioneers.

But surely L'Amour had written enough. Although he did not begin to publish under his own name until after he was 40, by the time of his death, 104 of his books had been published, 200 million copies were in print, and he was a multimillionaire with four homes (in California and Colorado).

The 1985 edition of my *Louis L'Amour* proved popular enough to merit, in the eyes of my editors, a revision at this time as a memorial. Between the end of 1984, my first cutoff date, and the time of his death, L'Amour published 11 more books. Since then, 5 more have appeared. All of this makes a total of 109 L'Amour books. So there is ample new material.

L'Amour's widow, now in charge of the Louis D. and Katherine E. L'Amour 1983 Trust, promises new titles well into the 1990s. It is unlikely, however, that any L'Amour novel after *The Haunted Mesa* or any L'Amour short-story collection after *The Outlaws of Mesquite* will alter the contours of his literary reputation. L'Amour's features may not be set in Mount Rushmore stone, but his artistic virtues and deficiencies are now firmly evidenced. His high points are marked by *Hondo, Flint,* several Sackett novels, *Bendigo Shafter, The Lonesome Gods, The Walking Drum,* and *Last of the Breed,* more than by any of his short stories or by any of his novels after 1986.

In chapter 1 of *Louis L'Amour, Revised Edition* I describe L'Amour's life, taking advantage of recently available material. In chapter 2 I show the range of his formulaic and historical novels and also touch on his short stories, only about a fourth of which have been collected. In chapters 3, 4, 5, and 6 I move chronologically through L'Amour's astonishing array of novels, doing so with two main points in mind. First, L'Amour soon learned and capitalized on what his public wanted, and therefore his novels show too little variety from about 1950 to the late 1970s. Second, toward the end of his career he realized that he had been building new fictive structures with mainly old bricks, and henceforth he began to introduce new features where he could; the results were almost always admirable, even if they were only sometimes successful.

L'Amour's most memorable literary accomplishments are his sagas of the Sackett, Chantry, and Talon families in the New World that span a period of three centuries. In chapter 7 I concentrate on these multivolume mini-epics. They invite comparison with works by other novelists using historical backdrops, recurring characters, and Balzacian, Zolaesque, and Faulknerian family trees. L'Amour lived to complete 25 volumes of his various Sackett, Chantry, and Talon series. If he had been productive for another decade, he might almost have doubled this number.

Chapter 8 is devoted to aspects of L'Amour's literary style. His handling of settings, characters, structure, diction, and sources merits much praise. But L'Amour was so fast and facile in his output that I feel obliged to present samples of his compositional errors—with no undue disrespect, of course, toward the best-selling western writer of all time. In chapter 9 I discuss L'Amour's major obsessions: America's Old West, Indians, women, and giving his readers advice on how to live.

In my 1985 *Louis L'Amour* I thanked friends and colleagues who provided information, advice, and encouragement early in the 1980s. Now, with the early 1990s upon us, let me thank or thank again my associates at the University of Pittsburgh David Brumble, Bruce Dobler, Edwin Marrs, and William L. Smith, my LaMoore family correspondents Edna LaMoore Waldo and Annabelle LaMoore (Mrs. Rodney S.) Shindo, my Library of Congress pen pal Ernest J. Parent, my friendly historian Carmen DiCiccio, western writer S. Jean Mead, my daughter Christine Gale, and my Twayne editors Jacob Conrad, Liz

Fowler, Carla Thompson, and Warren French—all for much-appreci-
ated professional courtesies. And, once again, my humble thanks to
my wife Maureen, who was born a few miles north of Skibbereen and
who shares with some of L'Amour's most intriguing characters the
enigmatic "Celtic gift."

Chronology

miere of movie *Shalako,* based on his novel of the same name, in London.

1969   Wins Golden Spur Award for *Down the Long Hills* (novel).

1971   *North to the Rails* (first Chantry novel); appears on "Merv Griffin" television show.

1972   Receives honorary doctorate in literature from Jamestown College, North Dakota.

1975   *Rivers West* (first Talon novel); appears on "Today" television show.

1976   Appears on "60 Minutes" television show.

1977   Receives Popular Culture Association Award of Excellence.

1978   Is awarded Great Seal of the Ute Tribe.

1979   *The Sacketts,* television miniseries.

1980   Tours country for three weeks aboard a bus rented by Bantam as part of promotion tour and celebration of 100 million L'Amour paperbacks in print.

1981   Is given Buffalo Bill and National Genealogical Society awards.

1982   Is voted National Gold Medal by U.S. Congress.

1983   Bantam decides to publish L'Amour in hardcover.

1984   Is awarded U.S. government Medal of Freedom; receives honorary doctorate from Pepperdine University, Malibu, California; appears on "Today" television show.

1985   Takes research trip to France and Thailand to work on *The Walking Drum* (novel).

1988   Dies 10 June, in Los Angeles home; *Lonigan* (short-story collection) and *A Sackett Companion* published posthumously; honorary doctorate awarded posthumously by Bowling Green State University, Bowling Green, Ohio.

1989   *Long Ride Home* (short-story collection) and *Education of a Wandering Man* (autobiography).

1990   *The Outlaws of Mesquite* (short-story collection).

1991   *The Rustlers of West Fork* (novel) is reissued as by L'Amour; 225 million copies of his books are in print worldwide.

Chapter One

Life of L'Amour

Louis L'Amour may be unique among the 15 or 20 most popular writers of western fiction, because details of his personal life have a strong bearing on his writing. The lives of his peers, inferiors, and superiors in the genre are usually of little consequence to their fiction, for their novels and short stories are mostly cast back in the nineteenth century, well before they were even born.

Does it matter to their writing and their readers that Henry W. Allen exercised polo ponies for Hollywood's moguls? That James Warner Bellah served in the U.S. Army in post–World War I Poland? That Matt Braun was a corporate journalist for a dozen years? That Walter Van Tilburg Clark was born in Maine and taught English? That Frederick Faust, a.k.a. Max Brand et al., preferred medieval romance literature to western fiction? That Zane Grey mixed dentistry and baseball before coloring any sage purple? That Ernest Haycox was a soldier and then a writer of rejected sea fiction? To continue—Dorothy Johnson typed, edited, and taught school; Frederick Manfred was a tall basketball player; Conrad Richter considered the ministry, clerked in a bank, and was a salesman; Jack Schaefer studied Latin and Greek and was a prison employee; Frank Waters was a petroleum and telephone engineer; and Owen Wister was a musician, banker, and lawyer before he went to where the west was west.

But with L'Amour, it is different. Everything he did before he became a western writer seems to have been "grist for his mill," to use one of his favorite clichés. As he explains in *Education of a Wandering Man,* "I am probably the last writer who will ever have known the people who lived the frontier life. In drifting about across the West, I have known five men and two women who knew Billy the Kid, two who rode in the Tonto Basin war in Arizona, and a variety of others who were outlaws, or frontier marshals like Jeff Milton, Bill Tilghman, and Chris Madsen, or just pioneers. I hear from some of their relatives from time to time, and it is always a pleasure."[1]

Early Life

In January 1946 World War II ex–army officer Louis Dearborn L'Amour went to a party in New York attended by copy-hungry editors and publishers. One of them had heard that L'Amour was determined to write for a living and invited him to send westerns to his pulp magazines, *Texas Rangers* and *Thrilling Ranch Stories.* Thus did the most phenomenal star of this pop-art form get his start—but success came only after years of hard work and much growth.

L'Amour was always happy to trace his American ancestry back to the 1630s, into New Hampshire, Virginia, and elsewhere. He was proud that in his veins ran English, Irish, French, and Canadian blood.[2] He was also pleased to follow his wife's English and Scottish roots far back in time. In fact, he contended in a 1973 interview that both sets of ancestors had once lived in the same small town of less than three thousand people and must, therefore, have known each other.[3] If so, these antecedents would resemble his intertwining fictional Sacketts, Chantrys, and Talons, concerning whom he has said: "As they move westward in different generations they brush elbows with each other and intermarry over a period of 40 years" (Bannon, 56). Later he adds: "In the stories of the Sacketts, Chantrys, and Talons . . . there are casual meetings between the families" (*Companion,* 11).[4]

L'Amour often mentioned the pioneering, fighting spirit of his forebears. His paternal grandfather, Robert L'Moore, was born in Ontario, fought in the Civil War (changing his name to Moore), returned home, and met and married a French-Canadian woman named Angeline LeDoux from the Montreal area.[5] They settled in Michigan. Their son, Louis Charles LaMoore, L'Amour's father, had a twin sister, both born 29 February 1868 at Marlette, Michigan. When he lost both that sister and their mother early in his life, he was sent to the home of his paternal grandfather. This man, who had a long line of Huguenot ancestors in northern Ireland, was a country doctor in Corinth, Ontario. His wife was Scottish. Young Louis Charles LaMoore returned to Marlette at about age 12, left at age 14 for Ellendale (now in North Dakota), and attended school there and at the Dakota Wesleyan Academy at Mitchell (now in South Dakota). He studied veterinarian medicine at the University of Toronto during the 1880s, and he moved to Jamestown, North Dakota, about 1890.[6]

One of L'Amour's great-grandfathers on his mother's side was Ambrose Freeman, an antislavery Virginian who moved to Illinois and then to St. Cloud, Minnesota, with his family. In 1862 he commanded rangers in skirmishes against the Sioux, and a year later he took part in the Sibley expedition, during which he was killed and scalped near the present location of Pettibone, North Dakota.[7] Another maternal L'Amour antecedent was Abraham Truman Dearborn, born in Susquehanna County, Pennsylvania. His New Hampshire–born father was of English stock; his mother was born in the Netherlands. Abraham Dearborn moved to Minnesota sometime before 1860, acquired land near West Union, and fought during the Civil War until his unit surrendered in 1862 at Murfreesboro, Tennessee. He was paroled to return home and fight Indians. While on the Dakota-Minnesota border, he met Ambrose Freeman. Freeman invited Dearborn to his home in St. Cloud, where he offered the young man hospitality and introduced him to his oldest daughter, Elizabeth "Betty" Freeman.[8] Dearborn returned to the South later in 1862 to fight in several more Civil War battles, was wounded in 1863 at or near Chickamauga, and went home to convalesce.[9] Meanwhile, Betty Freeman (whose father had died at the hands of the Sioux) went to her aunt's home in Paris, Illinois, married Abraham Dearborn there in 1864, and lived with him at Fort Halleck, Columbus, Kentucky, until after the Civil War ended. Subsequently, they farmed in Minnesota, had five children, and moved to the Dakota Territory in 1883. There, in Carrington, Dearborn worked for a land company and his wife kept a boardinghouse; in 1884, they moved to Jamestown, where he did carpentry work. Their third daughter, Emily Lavisa Dearborn (1870–1954), became the mother of Louis L'Amour.

It was in Jamestown that Emily met Louis Charles LaMoore. The two were married in 1892. After having six older children, two of whom died in infancy and one as a teenager, the couple welcomed Louis, the future novelist, to the family. His siblings were Edna May LaMoore Waldo (born 1893), (Charles) Parker LaMoore (1897–1954), Yale Freeman LaMoore (1899–1954), Emmy Lou LaMoore (1901–19; died during the influenza epidemic), and Clara and Clarice LaMoore (twins, 1903–1904).[10]

Louis Dearborn L'Amour was born on 22 March 1908. For some reason he was always vague, evasive, and even secretive about his age. He told one reporter, in 1980, "I spent my first years making people think I was older than I really was; now I'm working just as hard at keeping people from guessing my age." He told another reporter, in

1987, "I conscientiously object to anyone telling his age. . . . You can't judge people by age."[11]

L'Amour's father, known as Doc LaMoore, was a veterinarian in private practice and for the state of North Dakota, was chief of police in Jamestown, taught Sunday school in the Methodist church, was a local juvenile commissioner, and served as a town alderman and as a county and state delegate for the Republican party. He was sturdy, athletic— he taught his sons to box—temperate, and colorful. His daughter Edna recalls that he "was passionately fond of horses and dogs and raised both" (Waldo, "LaMoore Family"). When farm-working tractors began to put horses out to pasture, Doc LaMoore turned to selling and repairing steam threshers.[12] Emily LaMoore, L'Amour's mother, who was also called "Emma" and "Em," studied at the normal school in St. Cloud and planned to be a teacher, but married instead. She was always remembered as a quiet person, a passionate gardener, an avid reader, and a splendid storyteller. L'Amour apparently inherited a combination of physical strength and intelligent sensitivity from his wonderfully well-suited parents.

From the start, L'Amour was a blend of Huck Finn–like physicality and Tom Sawyer–like bookishness. Although he disliked school discipline, he attended classes as a youngster; however, at age 12 he decided that school was interfering with his education—and repeatedly said so.[13] While continuing to attend school until he was 15, he preferred both the outdoors and eclectic reading, not only in his family's small home library but also in the local town library (Klaschus, 12, 13; Gonzalez, 26). L'Amour says, "We probably had no more than two or three hundred books in my home when I was a child" (Education, 15).[14] The following partial list of his favorite reading, gleaned from many sources, is revealing: Balzac, Bulwer-Lytton, Chaucer, Conrad, Dickens, Dostoyevski, Dumas, Zane Grey, O. Henry, G. A. Henty, Hugo, Robinson Jeffers, Jack London, Longfellow, Marx, de Maupassant, John Stuart Mill, Nietzsche, Eugene O'Neill, Poe, Sir Walter Scott, Shakespeare, George Bernard Shaw, Robert Louis Stevenson, Tolstoy, Trollope, and H. G. Wells. Much later, L'Amour found the reading of most use to him professionally—western diaries, journals, newspapers, and history books and essays. It would be as much of a mistake to regard L'Amour as a rugged outdoors type who did not read as it would be to say that Ernest Hemingway, because of his adventuresome life in the 1920s and later, was not especially literate (Gonzalez, 24, 26).[15]

"Knockabout" Years

When L'Amour was 15, he knew nothing of the "glitterati" of the roaring Twenties. Indeed, in most areas of America, especially in the Midwest, many families in that decade and immediately thereafter experienced hardship at least and economic ruin at worst. The LaMoores, as they agreed to call themselves beginning about 1910 or a little later (Waldo, "LaMoore Family"; *Century,* 54), were no exception. With the advent of farm machinery, Doc LaMoore found himself in straitened circumstances. So he and his family, in December 1923, sold out in North Dakota, intending to head west for Oregon; but instead they detoured to visit Parker, already in Oklahoma City. After briefly accepting his older brother's hospitality, young Louis struck out on his own, beginning in January 1924.[16] He then began an incredible sequence of highly educative jobs, which all became "grist" for that future mill of his.[17]

Through essays about L'Amour and interviews with him, the public was treated to details that gradually coalesced into nothing less than a L'Amour legend. Harold E. Hinds, Jr., prefaces an essay on L'Amour with a summary of his subject's early career:

During the Depression [actually 1923] he [L'Amour] quit school when he was 15, and by the time he was 19 he had skinned cattle in Texas, lived with bandits in Sinkiang and Tibet, and served as second mate on an East Indian schooner. Over the years he tried his hand at a wide variety of picaresque occupations, among them professional boxer, longshoreman, lumberjack, elephant handler, fruit picker, hay schocker, gold prospector, and tank officer during World War II. In short, he was a jack-of-all-trades, the self-reliant man who could survive on any frontier.[18]

An interviewer augments the record thus:

L'Amour hopped freights, boxed in many prize fight rings, spent more than a few nights sleeping in jails, earned breakfast money handling circus elephants and eventually went to sea. He jumped ship in China where he knocked around the Far East in the days of the warlords and Japan's first military campaigns against its nearest Asian neighbor, living with bandits in Tibet and Sinkiang.

When World War II erupted, L'Amour was told he would be placed in navy intelligence where his knowledge of the Far East and Oriental languages would be useful. Instead, he found himself in Army khaki. Eventually he was made officer [in charge] of a tank destroyer, and he finished up the war in Europe after [reputedly—see note] fighting ashore on D-Day by commanding a platoon of the "Red Ball Express," the legendary unit of oil tankers that barreled along behind [General George S.] Patton's armor, bringing up the fuel the cavalry brigades gulped down to keep advancing. (Gonzalez, 24)[19]

L'Amour's last in-depth interviewer adds that L'Amour won $1,800 in a professional boxing match in Singapore, "saw criminals beheaded in China, biked across India . . . and survived a shipwreck in the West Indies," held his own in street fights in Shanghai and Bombay and Capetown, was a mine-assessment worker in the West, and was a beachcomber in San Pedro, California (Jackson, 164; see also Widener, 9–10).

Further, beginning with the publication of *The Broken Gun* in 1966, Bantam Books, L'Amour's lucky publisher, has made it a practice to include "About the Author" fillers, in which still more of his exploits are revealed—to the effect that he lectured widely, studied archaeology, compiled biographies of a thousand western gunfighters, sailed a dhow on the Red Sea, was shipwrecked in the West Indies, was stranded in the Mojave Desert, won 51 of 59 professional prizefights, pinch-hit for vacationing columnist Dorothy Kilgallen, and could count 33 writers among his family members.[20]

Thus, the years from L'Amour's leaving home until the end of World War II were varied and exciting. Still, many details are lacking and are likely to remain so, and some exploits may be legendary. For example, fans and critics alike would have welcomed cameo autobiographical narratives of his being taken for a horseback ride by Buffalo Bill, who L'Amour said "smelled slightly of bourbon and tobacco" (Widener, 10), and of his meeting famed Bill Tilghman and observing and then emulating his marksmanship.[21] They would also have liked more information concerning his professional boxing prowess, honest accounts of his maritime and his military activities, and more than teasing hints about romances on three continents.[22] Other interesting details about L'Amour's life are missing: for example, the truth about his relationship with his parents and with his siblings, Edna, Parker, and Yale; and an explanation of why he, like novelists Nathaniel Hawthorne, Herman Melville, and William Faulkner before him, saw fit to change the spelling of his last name.[23]

To be sure, with the advent of L'Amour's phenomenal popularity, additional tidbits of information about this best-selling author have turned up here and there. For example, when L'Amour returned from the sea, he associated informally with writing teachers and other people at the University of Oklahoma in Norman, broke into print as a book reviewer, and gathered some of his published verse into his first book, called *Smoke from This Altar*. The first edition of this book is now a collector's item but amounts to little more than juvenile versifying ("Scrapbook"; Klauchus, 14–15, 27–28; Hubbell, 96).[24]

After the War

In 1946 L'Amour decided to live in Los Angeles and write westerns. At that time, westerns were the most popular reading fare with the American public, which also had an insatiable appetite for western movies—and a little later for western television series as well.

At first, L'Amour tried routine western short stories, with pulp and then slick publishers. Just over a hundred such stories have been reprinted in the following Bantam collections: *War Party* (1975), *The Strong Shall Live* (1980), *Buckskin Run* (1980), *Bowdrie* (1983), *Law of the Desert Born* (1983), *Bowdrie's Law* (1984), *Dutchman's Flat* (11 old stories, 2 of which have characters named Bush and Quayle; 1986), *Riding for the Brand* (1986), *The Rider of the Ruby Hills* (1986), *The Trail to Crazy Man* (1986), *Lonigan* (1988), *Long Ride Home* (1989), and *The Outlaws of Mesquite* (1990). These stories mainly date from 1946 through the 1950s. Seven of them (novellas in *The Rider of the Ruby Hills* and *The Trail to Crazy Man*) L'Amour expanded into novels. During this early postwar period, he seems not to have been certain that westerns should be his métier. He was writing hard-boiled detective fiction as well, as evidenced by the 8 stories collected in *The Hills of Homicide* (1983), which reprints work first published in pulps in 1947–52. He also wrote some weak stories as early as 1938 about sea and war adventures, some 28 of which were republished in *Yondering* (1980), *Night over the Solomons* (1986), and *West from Singapore* (1987). The figure most often given for the total number of L'Amour's short stories is about 400, published in some 80 magazines in the United States and abroad.

In 1950 L'Amour published his first western novel, *Westward the Tide,* in England, strangely enough. It soon dropped out of sight, although it is commendable and introduces many of its author's central themes. A curious diffidence in L'Amour then appeared. He published

four Hopalong Cassidy books through Doubleday from 1950 through
1952 under the name Tex Burns. He also published *Showdown at Yellow
Butte* (1953; original short-story version, "Showdown on the Hog-
back," reprinted in *The Trail to Crazy Man*) and *Utah Blaine* (1954),
both under the name Jim Mayo.[25] The less said the better about the
quality of Tex Burns's efforts; but Jim Mayo's *Showdown at Yellow Butte*
and *Utah Blaine* are respectable action novels, especially the latter.[26]

   Then L'Amour published "The Gift of Cochise" in *Collier's* (5 July
1952).[27] Its success was the first of three major turning points in his
career. (The second was his marriage, and its stabilizing effect, in
1956; the third, Bantam's profitable decision to publish his books in
hardcover in 1983.) A year after publishing "The Gift of Cochise"
L'Amour expanded its crisp, fresh plot into the novel *Hondo*. The publisher, Fawcett, ballyhooed it well, printed 320,000 copies right off,
and propelled L'Amour to fame at once and to Bantam soon thereafter.[28] The story was turned into an exciting movie starring John
Wayne, Geraldine Page, Ward Bond, and James Arness (Warner,
1953). Long after, L'Amour lamented selling the film rights for a mere
$4,000.[29]

Promoting L'Amour

   Sales figures of works by L'Amour strain credulity. He is the most
phenomenally selling western writer of all time. *Hondo* is his best-
seller, with sales now well over 2.5 million copies. His *Sackett* and *Flint*
follow, having sold more than 2 million copies each. Then come *Silver
Canyon*, *The First Fast Draw*, *The Burning Hills*, *The Daybreakers*, *The
Sackett Brand*, *Mojave Crossing*, and *Lando*—each just under or just over
2 million copies.[30] According to Bantam publicity, each of his 87 novels is in print and sales of each have topped a million. In 1975 Bantam
crowed that L'Amour had surpassed their previous best-selling author
in paperback, John Steinbeck, whose 41.3 million–copy record is
nothing compared to their new leader's chart, from 50 million copies
in 1976 to more than 225 million in 1991. Especially staggering was
the 1985 Bantam statement on the dust jacket of the hardcover *Jubal
Sackett* that more than 30 million copies of the 17 volumes of the Sackett family saga were in print. In a good decade, L'Amour books might
sell at the rate of 15,000–20,000 copies a day—seven days a week. If
all the L'Amour books in print were stacked on top of one another,
they would reach more than 1,500 miles into space.[31]

Quality alone could not guarantee such success. In 1980 one of the most garish gimmicks in publishing history was put on wheels. It was "The Louis L'Amour Overland Express," a 1972 Luxury Custom Silver Eagle bus, complete with bedroom, sitting room, refrigerator, sofa, television, and other electronic gear. This monstrosity was leased by Bantam from a Nashville company that normally seeks its clientele among country and rock singers and bands, not mere writers. For three weeks in June, L'Amour cruised from Chicago to Moline, Rock Island, Davenport, Des Moines, Omaha, Kansas City, Tulsa, and Oklahoma City, hawking his fictive wares, meeting fans, and interminably signing copies of his 75 titles then available.[32] Nor had the moviemakers been idle. Beginning with *Hondo,* some 25 works by L'Amour have inspired movies and television adaptations. The best include *Guns of the Timberland* (starring Alan Ladd), 1960; *Heller in Pink Tights* (based on *Heller with a Gun* and starring Sophia Loren and Anthony Quinn), 1960; *Shalako* (starring Sean Connery and Brigitte Bardot), 1968; and *Catlow* (starring Yul Brynner, Richard Crenna, and Leonard Nimoy), 1971. The star-studded movie *How the West Was Won,* MGM's marvelous 1962 Cinerama epic, began as James R. Webb's screenplay, which L'Amour then converted into the 1963 novel.

The electronic media got into the act soon enough. A TV series based on *Hondo* was produced and telecast in 1967–68. Beginning in 1979 a miniseries called *The Sacketts,* based on *The Daybreakers* and *Sackett* together, L'Amour's first two Sackett-saga novels, enjoyed repeated success. In 1982 *The Cherokee Trail* appeared on TV, as did *The Shadow Riders.* In 1987 *The Quick and the Dead* and *Down the Long Hills* were shown on TV. In 1991 *Conagher* appeared on TV, starring Sam Elliott and his wife Katharine Ross and featuring L'Amour's attractive daughter Angelique in a bit part.[33] For good measure, Bantam in 1986 began to market audiocassettes of more than 30 of L'Amour's short stories, most of which were rendered quite exciting by introductory remarks by L'Amour, voices of fine professional actors such as Richard Crenna, and authentic sound effects. In addition, L'Amour appeared to great advantage on the popular CBS TV show "60 Minutes" in 1976; and, shortly after his death, his widow and his daughter were heard on Larry King's radio talk show.

L'Amour is tremendously popular abroad. His fiction has been translated into at least 20 foreign languages so far, including Chinese, Danish, Dutch, Finnish, French, German, Greek, Italian, Japanese, Norwegian, Polynesian, Portuguese, Serbo-Croatian, Spanish,[34] and

Swedish. Without a doubt, L'Amour has supplanted Zane Grey, Max Brand, Ernest Haycox, Luke Short, and Henry W. Allen as the most popular American western novelist in the eyes of foreign readers. In a thoughtful essay on recent western novels, Richard S. Wheeler has identified a bedrock virtue of L'Amour. Wheeler calls it "the absence of *anomie*," a term popularized by David Reisman's *The Lonely Crowd*. Anomie is variously defined as "social disconnectedness," "loss of social values," and "disorientation and social isolation." Wheeler concludes: "Louis L'Amour's stories remained free of anomie. His heroes and heroines were intimately and warmly connected with others. They cared about right and wrong and believed in traditional virtues—loyalty, courage, and honor."[35] L'Amour restored a sense of human family.

Personal Life

On 19 February 1956 in the grand ballroom of the Los Angeles Beverly Hilton, Louis L'Amour married Katherine Elizabeth (Keiner) Adams, a beautiful, savvy young woman who voluntarily quit a promising career as a TV actress to become Kathy L'Amour. The marriage was the first for each. The couple honeymooned in the West Indies and on the northern coast of South America. Of his marriage L'Amour once said, "That . . . is when I *really* struck it rich!" (Hubbell, 98). Born and educated in Los Angeles, and 26 years younger than her husband, Kathy was the daughter of a deceased real-estate developer and his actress wife (who in a later marriage became Mrs. Adams) and had appeared on episodes of "Gunsmoke" and "Death Valley Days." L'Amour averred that he was once engaged to Guitou de Felcourt, a widowed French countess with two children, and that actress Julie Newmar, to whom he was also allegedly engaged, introduced him to Kathy. For more than three decades, Kathy handled L'Amour family matters: house, children, servants, garden, correspondence, automobiles, travel plans, and financial and tax details.[36] The enormously wealthy L'Amours eventually owned a plush Los Angeles home, California ranch property, and two Colorado condominiums.[37] The L'Amours had one son, Beau Dearborn L'Amour, born in 1961, and one daughter, Angelique Gabrielle L'Amour, born in 1964.

The L'Amour home has been described by guests as a rambling, Spanish-style adobe hacienda on a quarter-block off Sunset Boulevard, complete with patios, gardens, pool, huge living room with fireplace, and study wing. This wing includes a workroom with a high ceiling lighted by a rosette window. The house is decorated with Indian rugs, paintings, dolls, mounted longhorns, original paintings first used as covers for many L'Amour best-sellers, a portrait of the author, and hinged double shelves for his much-vaunted library. There is even an adjacent gymnasium.[38]

L'Amour habitually followed a spartan, seven-day-a-week regimen. He rose early and infallibly put in a six-hour, two-fingered stint at one or both of his two electric typewriters; then, if production seemed satisfactory—5 to 10 pages a day, thus guaranteeing at least 35 pages a week—he would have lunch with friends (often in Beverly Hills) and then a workout with a punching bag, a stationary bike, and weights (Kalter, 7; Gonzalez, 26; Lee, 50; Jackson, 160, 170).[39] L'Amour made many peculiar statements about his writing technique. He boasted that he never rewrote anything (Widener, 14),[40] which is both obvious and regrettable. He also claimed that he "never dash[ed] off a quickie" (Kalter, 4), which is not true. Also, he confessed to one reporter that he believed an author "usually doesn't have the faintest idea what's going to happen to the characters in his books. He just puts them somewhere and sees what happens" (Widener, 14). To another reporter he amplified: "I start with a character and a situation, but I don't know what's going to happen until I write it. Sometimes things happen that surprise me" (Jackson, 170). Until his last few years, L'Amour lectured widely, traveled tirelessly—in Canada, Europe, and the Far East, but mainly in the United States—to find new material and haunt old locales again, and even scouted scenes with hired drivers and on foot with guides, by four-wheeler, and by airplane and helicopter—some of the time with his son Beau as cameraman (McDowell, 34).[41]

L'Amour should remain an inspiration for people who are tempted to give up and chronically relax before they are "old." In 1973 he expressed the hope that he would sell 40–60 million books in the following decade (Bannon, 57). He did better than that. In 1979 a reporter sketched L'Amour thus: "His bulwark of a chest has caved in only slightly into his belly, and his six-foot frame [make that 6-foot, 1-inch frame, at 215 pounds] is unbent despite its nearly 70 [make that 71] years of wear" (Nuwer, 99). In 1980 L'Amour informed another reporter that he had 34 plots outlined and on his desk (Reed, 108) and added to another interviewer that he had plans for 40 more Sackett, Chantry, and Talon novels (Gonzalez, 25–26). In 1982 another reporter described L'Amour's bulletin board as festooned with scribbled ideas for "at least forty-five . . . novels in the making" (Ring, 48). In 1986 the number was back down to 34 (Chan, 4). L'Amour was insatiable in his hunger for readers. He said to one interviewer, "There are at least 25 million readers out there that I've never touched at all . . . and I want them—I want every damned one of them" (Gonzalez, 22). To another he confided: "It's nice to think when you are flying in a plane and you look down there and see the lights, you can almost bet that somebody is reading one of your books. It's a nice feeling."[42]

An aspect of L'Amour's pugnaciousness surfaced in 1983, when the New York publishers Carroll & Graf announced plans to issue *The Hills of Homicide* and *Law of the Desert Born,* collecting early stories by L'Amour that he had neglected to recopyright. After a messy lawsuit brought by L'Amour in New York, Carroll & Graf was allowed to proceed but only after altering promotional material and paperback-cover artwork. Meanwhile, L'Amour pressured Bantam to rush into print his "authorized" versions of the same stories with identical cover titles, plus some extra stories, plus trivial prefatory and annotative material hastily slapped together.[43] Unbelievably, Carroll & Graf in 1986 poached once more on L'Amour's little acre of public domain and bagged enough L'Amour stories for two more books. And, once again, L'Amour flung out two more collections, *Riding for the Brand* and *Dutchman's Flat,* again with duplicate contents and then some, including dull prefaces and introductions.[44]

Now for some more pleasant notes. Back in the 1960s, L'Amour began to make some admirable plans for the re-creation of an 1865 authentic western town, to be called Shalako, and to be located just west of Durango, where Arizona, Colorado, New Mexico, and Utah meet. Shalako was to have been a working town, movie location, and tourist attraction. The work "shalako," as the titular hero of L'Amour's novel *Shalako* explains to the heroine, is the "name of the Zuni rain god." Then he adds, "Seems like every time I showed up in their country it rained, so they called me that for a joke."[45] Bantam publicity kept this project before the public for years. Blurbs about the town of Shalako continued on "About the Author" pages in L'Amour paperbacks until 1984, then stopped. Problems raised by environmentalists and utility companies delayed and then quashed construction. L'Amour's last word on the subject of Shalako appears in *The Sackett*

Companion: "Plans do not always come to fruition, . . . and these plans were dependent upon others than myself" (177).

In August 1982 the U.S. Congress voted to award L'Amour a special gold medal, while also awarding similar medals to musician Fred Waring and to the widow of prizefighter Joe Louis. L'Amour was honored for his chronicling of the settlement of the west. President Ronald Reagan presented the medal at a White House ceremony on 24 September 1983, calling attention at that time to the recipient's "enormous contributions to western folklore and our frontier heritage."[46] The irrepressible L'Amour is quoted as earlier lamenting the fact that Reagan never appeared in a movie based on one of his stories. "Maybe I can talk him into doing one some day," he added.[47] Almost anticlimactically, L'Amour appeared at the White House again, on 26 March 1984, to accept the American government's highest civilian award, the Presidential Medal of Freedom, for his fiction dramatizing the American pioneering spirit.[48]

Final Years

L'Amour's last six years were crammed with activity, honors, and successes, as befitted such a vigorous and productive man. He continued to travel, though less than in former years. He lectured and was given honorary degrees. He also published 8 novels, 10 collections of short stories, and a book about his Sackett saga. He also drafted what became his posthumously published memoir, *Education of a Wandering Man*.

Beginning with *The Lonesome Gods* in 1983, Bantam went hardcover with many of L'Amour's books—and with spectacular sales successes. When *The Walking Drum* (1984), *Jubal Sackett* (1985), *Last of the Breed* (1986), *The Haunted Mesa* (1987), and *The Outlaws of Mesquite* (1990) were all issued in hardcover, Bantam cornered with each a part of the best-seller hardcover market, then paused, then reissued the titles in paperbacks, which also became best-sellers all over again. It must have delighted reader-hungry L'Amour that in every year from 1983 through 1987 two or more of his books were on best-seller lists simultaneously. Less pleasing to him, in all probability, were many of the reviews. L'Amour had long griped that critics did not take his writing seriously because it appeared in paperback. Once in hardcover, however, his novels were more thoroughly, and often more adversely, scrutinized. So L'Amour changed his attitude and began to say that he did not care what the critics had to say, since his public remained devoted.

L'Amour regularly avoided talk about royalties: "Just say I'm very successful," he told an interviewer in 1986 (Chan, 4). Bantam still declines to release monetary figures. But juggling touted printing totals, one may conservatively estimate that for the new titles he published between 1983 and 1988 L'Amour enjoyed royalties totaling $12 to $15 million, and this figure does not include continuing sales of most of his 85 pre-1983 books and all of his numerous audiocassettes, produced by Beau L'Amour, along with steadily selling annual calendars, which could together have easily added $12 to $15 million more.[49]

In the year of his death, L'Amour even helped his daughter Angelique to put together an anthology of maxims, aphorisms, and clichés culled from his fiction. This 1988 work, called *The Trail of Memories: The Quotations of Louis L'Amour,* is divided into two dozen categories (for example, "Life," "Women," "Time," "Indians," "Trust," and "Death") and contains many nice nuggets but overall too much dusty sand. It really should never have been published.[50] More commendable was L'Amour's own 1988 effort, called *The Sackett Companion: A Personal Guide to the Sackett Novels.* This useful tome provides encyclopedic details of the backgrounds and sources of his nine-generation Sackett saga, which only death kept him from extending far beyond its 17-volume limit. Crying out for continuations too were both *The Walking Drum* and *Last of the Breed.* But death buried them as well, although L'Amour evidently did considerable research toward *Drum* sequels.

The last new work by L'Amour, and one that might have been illuminating had he finished it, was *Education of a Wandering Man.* Although press releases and comments by his widow would have it that he was proofreading it only hours before he died,[51] in truth he left it in dreadful shape and it is obvious that disparate sections of it must have been pasted together later by others. Clearly, L'Amour was near death as he drafted this work, for it was unlike him to write such lines as these, which actually appear in it: "Time may not be allowed me," "when I go down that last trail," and "this wandering man, who has ceased to wander except in his memory, his thoughts, and the books he writes" (116, 142, 166).

Louis L'Amour died in his Los Angeles home on 10 June 1988. The cause of death was given as lung cancer. Obituaries noted that the world-famous author, a nonsmoker, might have developed the disease as a result of working in mines in his youth.[52]

Late in his enviably full and varied life, L'Amour put the following peculiar promise in writing: "I shall do an autobiography, perhaps as fiction—which I write best—but it will be true" (*Education*, 168). It would surely have been another curious combination of fact and legend, but death prevented his offering it to his readers.[53] Before choosing *Education of a Wandering Man* as the title of his most nearly autobiographical book, L'Amour thought of calling it *Dusty Shoes*.[54]

Chapter Two
L'Amour's Range

Most L'Amour addicts probably read their favorite western fiction writer because of his elaborate plots. Along the road to various predictable climaxes, such buffs pause to enjoy the scenery, savor the dialogue, appreciate the advice and history lectures, and pause in surprise over the rare humor. Oddly, there is little violence; moreover, it is well controlled. Also, those who seek cheap sex scenes, such as those that fill so-called adult westerns, are advised to avoid L'Amour.[1]

Lots of Plots

L'Amour is best for his plots. He often remarked that he saw himself as a troubadour, a tale-teller, a campfire entertainer. He once reminded an interviewer that 90 percent of all fiction is based on 12 to 18 or so basic plots, and that the Greeks, Chaucer, Shakespeare, and Dickens all reworked the same formulas; then went on to recall that "George[s] Polti many years ago listed 36 basic plots and nobody has ever improved on his list" (Gonzalez, 24).[2] Like most other western storytellers, L'Amour employs few of Polti's situations, common ones being rivalry of superior and inferior, daring enterprise, criminal pursued by avenger, puzzlement, falling victim to cruelty, and rebellion. Polti would have been pleased to cite L'Amour's plots as illustrating rivalry over something of value, rescue missions, justice, and pursuit and capture.

Frank Gruber in *Pulp Jungle* identifies seven basic western plots: Union Pacific story, ranch story, empire story, revenge story, Custer's last stand, outlaw story, and marshal story.[3] L'Amour used all seven of these plot types. Here are examples. "Merrano of the Dry Country" (reprinted in *The Strong Shall Live*) tells how a man of superior qualities defeats not only a stubborn environment but also prejudice in a neighborhood of inferior rivals. Kilkenny, hero of "A Man Called Trent" (rewritten as *The Mountain Valley War* and reprinted in *The Rider of the Ruby Hills*), tries to homestead in Idaho but rides into a feud between cattlemen and farmers. *Ride the Dark Trail* presents a widow's defense against a villain's scheme to steal her ranch. The hero of *The Burning Hills* avenges his partner's murder. *Kilrone,* a variation of the Custer story, features an ex-army officer, a military post, and Indians. In *Son of a Wanted Man* (the original version being "The Trail to Peach Mountain Canyon," reprinted in *The Rider of the Ruby Hills*) an outlaw and his son try to reform, one late, the other just in time. And the lawdog in "The Marshal of Sentinel" (in *The Strong Shall Live*) defends his town, erases an old mistake, aids a drunkard, and impresses a woman.

L'Amour plays variations on the seven themes from Gruber. Here are examples. "Merrano of the Dry Country" is an early lecture on western ecological dangers. Kilkenny proved so popular that L'Amour featured him in other works. The widow in *Ride the Dark Trail* was a Sackett before marrying into the Talon family, and hence she connects this book with almost two dozen other L'Amour novels. *The Burning Hills* is a revenge story but also has racial elements provided by one of its author's few Hispanic heroines. Many L'Amour novels besides *Kilrone* dramatize clashes between whites and Indians; most of them avoid the tedium of "Custer's last stand" stereotypes. Often L'Amour introduces an ex-outlaw hero who tries hard to mend his ways. Occasionally, as in *Dark Canyon,* dirty criminal money stakes the reformed hero to a second chance. And one of the best marshal yarns by L'Amour is *Borden Chantry* (1977), which introduces Borden even though his murder was reported earlier in *North to the Rails* (1971).

L'Amour's most common plot has to do with land rivalry. *Utah Blaine, Kilkenny, Guns of the Timberlands, Silver Canyon, Flint, Over on the Dry Side,* several Sackett titles, and several short stories, including "West of the Tularosas" (reprinted in *Dutchman's Flat*), head a long list of such works. L'Amour has also written a number of novels concerned with mining and hidden treasure: for example, *Taggart, Lando, The High Graders, The Empty Land, Under the Sweetwater Rim, The Ferguson Rifle, Bendigo Shafter,* and *Comstock Lode.* There are also a few wagon-train novels, including *Westward the Tide* and *The Tall Stranger.* L'Amour seldom deals in a central way with gunmen, but *The First Fast Draw, High Lonesome,* and a few short stories, including "His Brother's Debt" (in *Riding for the Brand*), do so. A few of L'Amour's novels are about cattle drives and little else—for example, *Matagorda, Killoe,* and *Chancy.* Former detective-story writer L'Amour may be counted on to tangle a western hero in a who-done-it yarn, as in *Borden Chantry, The Iron Marshal, Milo Talon,* several short stories featuring durable Chick Bowdrie (in *Bowdrie* and *Bowdrie's Law*), and "Heritage of Hate" (in *Lonigan*). *Conagher* and *The Cherokee Trail* are stage-station westerns, as are some short stories, including "Alkali Basin" (in *War Party*) and "Bluff Creek Station" (in *The Strong Shall Live*). Several plots defy easy pigeonholing. For example, *Heller with a Gun* is about traveling actors and actresses in the west; *Sitka* is mostly about Alaska; *Fair Blows the Wind* is a swashbuckler; *The Lonesome Gods* is a veritable anthology of L'Amour special effects (to be discussed later); *The Haunted Mesa* is about crossing time barriers; "One Night Stand" (in *The Strong Shall Live*) is a spoof about an actor who impersonates Wild Bill Hickok; and "The Lion Hunter and the Lady" (in *Dutchman's Flat*) stars a catamount trapper.

Formula or History?

More instructive than Polti's or Gruber's plot categorizings is Jon Tuska's division of western fiction into three classes—formulary narrative, romantic historical reconstruction, and historical reconstruction. Tuska regards the first and third groups as distinct, with the second combining elements from the first and third (Tuska, 3–4).

The formulary western has been a beloved staple in popular culture for generations. John G. Cawelti first identified and analyzed the importance of setting, characters, and plot patterns in the formula. The setting is obviously western, usually beyond the Mississippi River, where distances are vast, water is scarce and valuable, and nature can be inimical, where sunlight glares and darkness is mitigated only by diamond-clear stars, but also where nature, if one surrenders to it, can be heart-stopping in its beauty. Character patterns in formulary western fiction are combinations of the following: savages, white and otherwise, some of whom go west to exploit the west and then leave, while others stay to revere the west and build; townspeople, including women, who aim to settle; and the lonely hero, typically a fellow with a shadowy past that need not matter now, habitually taciturn but capable of poetic utterance, adept with weapons and horses, and commonly wearing distinctive western garb. Women are a special subgroup. They began in western fiction as simple and pure heroines; later, they divided into heroines and "soiled doves"; still later, they were featured in pairs, almost equally good though so confusing as to give pause to the tardily amorous hero; recently, fictive western women have begun to be "liberated." "Savages" too have been characterized anew by revisionists; hence, bloodthirsty, rape-seeking "redskins" have been modified to include realistically noble Indians, who are credibly human, hence sometimes violent, but also more understandably motivated.[4]

Cawelti accepts plot complexities adumbrated by both Polti and Gruber, but he adds this valuable generalization, which subsumes at least Gruber's seven types:

> [a] basic situation . . . develops out of . . . the epic moment when the values . . . of American society stand balanced against the savage wilderness. The situation must involve a hero who possesses some of the urges toward violence as well as the skills, heroism and . . . honor ascribed to the wilderness way of life, and it must place this hero . . . where he becomes involved with . . . the agents and values of civilization. . . . [T]he conflict between town and wilderness . . . [implies] that the formulaic pattern of action is that of chase and pursuit because it is in this pattern that the clash of savages and townspeople manifests itself. (66–67)

Cawelti adds that the western is uniquely popular because its readers see in it "a brilliantly articulated game" with players on obviously opposite sides, restricted by rules permitting certain actions but not others, moving somewhat predictably toward an anticipated end, and all on a "board or field" marked with a kind of "line of scrimmage" (71). Players in this game are the characters, moves constitute plot elements, and the field may actually be a mountain, canyon, forest, plain, desert, trail, ranch, or saloon.

Tuska's third category, historical reconstruction, is "sound historical fiction" set in the American west and written to explain what happened in our past there. Tuska continues: "But the truth isn't always concerned with purely physical events; sometimes . . . it has to do with spiritual events. To reclaim . . . the spiritual past . . . is the primary objective." As is not the case with formularies, the hero of a historical reconstruction is "a human being . . . while the structure is expanded to encompass complexity of character and incident." Reading such works, "we come to recognize our solidarity with people from the past; we relive their lives, face the issues which confronted them, and . . . come to some deeper understanding of ourselves." Such fiction can be "stirring and entertaining and still be historically accurate, truthful to the time, the place, and the people" (19, 22, 23).

In his bibliography, Tuska lists many western historical reconstructions, but no works by L'Amour, who might well have been outraged at being excluded. It was his opinion that extensive historical research buttresses much of his formulary fiction and most of his historical novels and that he should qualify as a historical reconstructionist. Tuska would counter that L'Amour should have felt complimented enough to have his works fall into the category of romantic historical reconstruction. Tuska grants that this hybrid class is illustrated by fiction with characters having more depth and impelled by events having more complexity than is the case with formulary fiction. But he adds that romantic reconstructionists know little history and that they not only hold that modicum of history in contempt but also deceitfully entertain readers by failing to appeal to their conscience.

L'Amour's Formula

Why, then, has L'Amour been so incredibly popular? It would seem that formulary westerns are outmoded and that romantic historical reconstructions are vapid. The plain truth is that L'Amour is popular because he takes formulary and historical models and plays melodramatic variations on them. Also, in the well-worn tradition of Mark Twain and William Faulkner, he is a master of giving the impression that he is at a campfire or some other cozy place with his readers, swiftly characterizing his heroes and heroines and villains and subsidiary types in between, rushing them into action, and placing them in locales seemingly real and in times that may be gone but that his readers wish they could visit. L'Amour could never have succeeded if he had merely followed a stale recipe with the same old ingredients.

It should be recorded here that L'Amour's work was too popular and facile to deserve being defined as an absorbing critical challenge. Every serious chapter about him and every in-depth review of his novels underline this fact. It is regrettable that he did not try earlier in his career to branch out, be innovative, take a chance. He began to do so only with *The Walking Drum, Last of the Breed,* and *The Haunted Mesa.* But by the mid-1980s, when these novels were published, it was too late; in addition, the hero of each is really not much more than another L'Amour cowboy in disguise. It would also seem that L'Amour equated quantity with quality. He thought that he deserved critical accolades because of his sales figures. How else can one account for his boasting that he wrote *The Walking Drum* "15 years ago but my publisher got me to put it on the shelf. He didn't know what a favor he was doing me. . . . Because now it's worth a good deal more money than it was then" (Rogers, 4D).[5]

Time and Place

Two of L'Amour's most enduring attributes are his reconstructions of long-ago times and his evocation of faraway places. These strengths may be well illustrated by indicating the spread of his works through time, mainly in the nineteenth century, but often back into other centuries as well, and by mapping his geographic range, which sweeps over continents.

The earliest action in any L'Amour novel is that of a humble coyote in seventh-century pre-Utah. *The Empty Land* begins with a lecture on history: about Pope Gregory the Great, Ireland's golden age of scholarship, the Merovingian kings, the war between China and Champa (later known as South Vietnam), T'ang in China, and Mohammed in Mecca. More importantly for American civilization, L'Amour's seventh-century coyote dug into a chipmunk hole, and enlarged the opening for water and a juniper root, which grew and in time exposed gold—for a certain trapper to find in 1824.

The year 1824 is early for L'Amour but not by any means his earliest narrative date. *The Walking Drum* takes his readers back to late twelfth-century Europe and the Middle East, and he time-warps readers of *The Haunted Mesa* back to the thirteenth century in the American Southwest. Reminiscences in *Fair Blows the Wind* hark back to the 1570s in Ireland, and much action involving progenitor Tatton Chantry occurs before 1588. The earliest action in any Sackett novel occurs in 1599, when Barnabas Sackett, hero of *Sackett's Land,* leaves the Cambridge-shire fens for Elizabethan London to the south and then goes west across the Atlantic to the sparse Carolinas. *To the Far Blue Mountains* and *The Warrior's Path* fast-forward the action to 1630, and *Jubal Sackett* continues it immediately thereafter. L'Amour explains that the locale of Barnabas's New World home in Shooting Creek may now be found off the highway between Franklin, North Carolina, and Chattanooga, Tennessee, while his death site is in the mountains above Crab Orchard (Foreword to *Sackett Novels,* 1:viii; *Companion,* 55). Jubal bids his father Barnabas farewell, goes down what became the Mississippi River and up the Arkansas River, to the Rocky Mountains and then to the Far West. The Talon-family saga starts with Jean Talon leaving the gor-

geous Gaspé Peninsula in northeastern Canada in 1821, in search of
fame, fortune, and romance, and proceeding to Maine, Albany, Pittsburgh, St. Louis, and points west—all in *Rivers West*.
These Chantry, Sackett, and Talon family epics pose vexing time
problems. Some segments offer contrary evidence; others, insufficient.
L'Amour's *Sackett Companion* comments are of limited help and concern
the Chantrys and Talons only tangentially. L'Amour promised to carry
the histories of these families back into earlier periods and forward
into the twentieth century. But death cut his grand design short by
perhaps 20 volumes.

The action in all but two of L'Amour's other novels is in the nineteenth century and with few exceptions in the 1860s, 1870s, and
1880s. Major events in one Chantry novel, *The Ferguson Rifle*, occur
about 1804, although the story starts in North Carolina in 1780. Action in another Chantry book, *North to the Rails*, may transpire as late
as 1890, during a cattle drive out of Santa Fe, but this late date is the
consequence of carelessness on L'Amour's part. *The Tall Stranger*, the
beginning of *Sitka, Down the Long Hills*, most of *The Empty Land*, *The
Californios*, and *Ride the River* detail events cast in the 1840s. Action
in *Killoe*, *The Quick and the Dead*, and most of *The Lonesome Gods* may
be dated in the 1850s. L'Amour was inexplicably reluctant to describe
much western action immediately before the Civil War.

Furthermore, L'Amour did not set many narratives in the tragic
Civil War years, perhaps through fear of losing Southern readers because of his pro-Union sentiments as well as his forebears' Union army
activities. Most of his dozen or so 1860s novels start after the war.
True, *The Cherokee Trail* takes place mostly in 1864, but its central
character is the widow of a Civil War officer and has gone west to
manage a stagecoach station in Colorado. The hero of *Under the Sweetwater Rim*, the action of which is also to be dated 1864, is an army
officer who discomfits a villain supplying rifles to Indians between Fort
Laramie and Fort Bridger. L'Amour dates many of his 1860s novels by
alluding to the Civil War as recently ended. Examples include *Conagher*, *Callaghen*, and *The Iron Marshal*. In those works, as sometimes
elsewhere, he is precise as to the date. Thus, *The Shadow Riders* begins
exactly at the end of the war and carries its readers into southeastern
Texas, by the Gulf of Mexico. Action in *The Man from Skibbereen*,
placed in Wyoming Territory, is dated October 1868. Other examples
abound.

Action in about a third of L'Amour's novels occurs in the 1870s.

Thus, *Lonely on the Mountain*, since it features Louis Riel between the time of his rash rebellion in northwestern Canada and his escape from its consequences, must transpire in the summer of 1870. L'Amour explicitly dates *Chancy* 1871. Ulysses S. Grant is campaigning for re-election during the action of *Brionne*, the main events of which must necessarily occur in 1872. Sometimes L'Amour is more general. In *Mojave Crossing*, for example, he writes that the outlaw Tiburcio Vásquez (1835–75) was recently captured near tiny Los Angeles. In *Crossfire Trail* he states that General George Armstrong Custer is now in the Badlands, northeast of the fictive action. *Kilkenny* events occur after the death of Wild Bill Hickok (1837–76). Mention is made in *The Key-Lock Man* and *Son of a Wanted Man* of Jesse James's raid on Northfield, Minnesota (September 1876). Occasionally L'Amour taps out a precise date, as in *The Sackett Brand*, when narrator Tell Sackett, after burying his murdered wife, puts the date 25 April 1877 on her grave marker.

Novels detailing events in the 1880s are fewer in number than those concerned with the 1870s. *Taggart* is set in 1880; *Shalako*, in the spring of 1882. But the other half-dozen or so are only loosely datable. Thus, one can pin down the time of action in *The Mountain Valley War* in southwestern Idaho Territory only as between the death of Johnny Ringo (1844–82) and the admission of Idaho as a state (1890).

Only a few of L'Amour's novels narrate events spreading out over years, even decades. *Sitka* starts about 1845 in Pennsylvania, carries its hero to sea and even to Russia, and continues to the time of the Alaska Purchase (1867). *Reilly's Luck* starts in Montana about 1861 (although the Civil War goes unmentioned) with the hero a mere child of four, destined for picaresque episodes as far away as Europe; the story ends about 1882, since it is said that the town of Durango is two years old. *Bendigo Shafter* opens in 1859 and advances to the time of the enfranchisement of women in Wyoming (1870). *Comstock Lode* begins in Cornwall in 1849, with the hero a youngster whom the complex plot will take to adulthood in 1859, 1860, and 1861—with news of the Civil War reaching him in Nevada.

The action of a few L'Amour novels cannot be dated even within a decade. It would appear that such cowboy and frontier books dramatize events of the 1870s or thereabouts. Examples include *Utah Blaine*, *Guns of the Timberlands* (with an ex–Texas Ranger for hero), *The Burning Hills*, and *Fallon*.

Rather engagingly, L'Amour carries the action of a couple of his fictional pieces beyond the climax by means of thumbnail sketches of descendants of main characters. Thus, at the end of *Dark Canyon* he comments on a certain great-grandson killed during the Korean War. The hero of *The High Graders* is disappointed when his grandson joins a Madison Avenue advertising agency. So, too, in "Bluff Creek Station" (in *The Strong Shall Live*), at the end of which it is reported not only that a motel has now replaced the old stage station, but also that descendants of the hero died in the Argonne Forest, Normandy, and Vietnam.

Many of L'Amour's nonwestern short stories are set in the twentieth century, but only two western novels are: *The Broken Gun* and *The Haunted Mesa*. *The Broken Gun* is really a western that wandered beyond its proper time; it is narrated by and stars Dan Sheridan, one of L'Amour's most autobiographical heroes—200 pounds in weight, combat veteran (Korea and Vietnam), ex-boxer, successful writer and researcher, and man of action in the west (specifically Arizona) in 1962 or so. Mike Raglan, the hero of *The Haunted Mesa*, mentions seeing "two books by Evans-Wentz and one by Eliade."[6] This dates its action, since the two books in question are probably W. Y. Evans-Wentz's 1981 *Cuchama and Sacred Mountains* and the 1981 translation of Mircea Eliade's autobiography. Mike is also an autobiographical figure. Big and strong, he was an on-his-own teenager who did ranch, circus, and mining work, spent time in Tibet, studied Arabic, and became a writer in New York and Los Angeles. Finally, set in Siberia in 1985–86, *Last of the Breed* presents action in the most nearly contemporary era.

When asked in 1983 about the new frontier (space), twentieth-century technological cowboys (astronauts), and their latter-day steeds (space capsules), L'Amour replied that he had written no space fiction but then added, "I may. I've often thought about it. I certainly will do some writing on the subject" (Rogers, 4D). A few years later he grew more specific: "I am . . . concerned now (as I have been since I was twelve) about the frontiers of outer space . . . This is the final frontier, the frontier without end, and those who explore it will be the heroes of the future" (*Education*, 155).

Short-Fiction Time and Space

The action in most of L'Amour's reprinted western short stories, like that of his novels, dates roughly to between 1850 and 1885. The collections are *War Party, The Strong Shall Live, Buckskin Run, Bowdrie,*

Law of the Desert Born, Bowdrie's Law, Dutchman's Flat, Riding for the Brand, The Rider of the Ruby Hills, The Trail to Crazy Man, Lonigan, Long Ride Home, and *The Outlaws of Mesquite.* Many of the tales are rehearsals for later novels. "Trap of Gold" (in *War Party* and *Law of the Desert Born*) became part of *Taggart.* "War Party" (in *War Party*) was expanded into *Bendigo Shafter.* "Booty for a Bad Man" (in *War Party*) introduced readers to Tell Sackett. "The Gift of Cochise" (in *War Party*), itself prepared for by "Ride, You Tonto Raiders!" (in *Law of the Desert Born*), led to *Hondo* (as already noted). "Hattan's Castle" (in *The Strong Shall Live*) previewed *The Empty Land.* "Dutchman's Flat" (in *Dutchman's Flat*) was expanded into *The Key-Lock Man.* And "Home in the Valley" (in *Riding for the Brand*) provided an episode for *Sitka.*

The four other collections of L'Amour's short fiction are *Yondering, The Hills of Homicide, Night over the Solomons,* and *West from Singapore.* All of the stories in them are cast in the twentieth century and are hardly vintage L'Amour. He reissued them only to make money by capitalizing on his can't-miss popularity. None would have sold out a modest first printing if issued under either of his pen names. *Yondering* mostly features sea adventures in Far Eastern waters, in the 1920s and 1930s, and seems partly autobiographical. Thrown in for good measure are a couple of war stories, one concerning the Spanish foreign legion in the 1920s, another about freedom fighters against the Nazis in Greece in 1941. *The Hills of Homicide* presents 8 hard-boiled detective stories originally published in 1947–52 pulps and sketching contemporary seamy life. Only the title story, cast in and near Las Vegas, and a piece entitled "Stay Out of My Nightmare," set in Los Angeles, are worth more than a passing glance. Both are redolent of precolorized film noir, such as George Raft and Humphrey Bogart movies, and in their era might have done well if adapted for the screen. All six stories in *Night over the Solomons* concern free-lance, pro-democracy pilots fighting German and Japanese villains from the time of Pearl Harbor to the early days of the atomic age, mostly in the skies over the South Seas, Indonesia, South America, and Siberia and then down at ground, beach, and sea level. One of the stories, "Wings over Khabarovsk," prefigures *Last of the Breed.* The seven yarns spun *West from Singapore* star Ponga Jim Mayo, who owns a tramp freighter and plies Indonesian waters in search of profit, anti-Nazi and anti-Japanese adventure, but never romance. The 13 stories in *Night over the Solomons* and *West from Singapore* are notable for breakneck plots, gore undiluted by subtlety, and thin characterization. Every one of them has laughable stylistic flaws, while a few are so close to the slapstick idiocy of *Romancing the Stone* and the various Indiana Jones romps that probably only friendship or embarrassment stopped the L'Amour family from suing the Hollywood moguls responsible for those films. It should be added that in several of the stories L'Amour engagingly evokes the sights, sounds, and smells of faraway places—jungles, mountains, archipelagos, tropic waters, and starry skies—all of which, to judge by their vividness in these stories, he must have remembered until the end of his life with undiminished ecstasy.

Chapter Three
L'Amour at Dawn

The *New Western Magazine* of 6 August 1949 included a short story entitled "Ride, You Tonto Raiders!" by L'Amour. It is a near microcosm of the fictional west he subsequently created. The story dropped from sight until it was reprinted in the 1983 collection of stories entitled *Law of the Desert Born*.

Ingredients for Success

"Ride, You Tonto Raiders!" stars Mathurin Sabre. Matt is a former buffalo hunter, prospector in Mexico, revolutionist in Central America, foreign legionnaire in Morocco, vacationer in France and elsewhere, Texas trail herder, and marshal of Mobeetie, Texas. Tall, broad-shouldered, lightning-quick, he mortally wounds Billy Curtin in an El Paso gunfight, and Billy begs him to deliver some $5,000 to his widow, Jenny, who is ranching with their son Billy, Jr., in the Tonto Basin outside Yellowjacket, Arizona. Doing so, Matt learns that Prince McCarran covets Jenny's land and is aided by saloon and mine owner Galusha Reed, gunslinger Tony Sikes, and bumbling town marshal Sid Trumbull. Matt soon likes Jenny a lot, is understandably reluctant to explain how her husband died, and wants to save her spread. He is befriended by Simpson, a canny codger; stableman Camp Gordon, who is Cambridge-educated, drinks to excess, and spouts Shakespeare; a saloon piano player named Keys, who once knew Johann Strauss, Jr., in Vienna; old Tom Judson and half-breed Silerado ("Rado"), both of whom work for Jenny; and Pepito Fernandez, grandson of the Hispanic who sold Curtin his land.

More salient than plot, however, are the character types and stylistic features in this story. Half the stereotypical relationships and action of L'Amour's future fiction are visible right here. Matt's background previews that of a dozen later L'Amour heroes. Killing the man whose wife the hero will later marry anticipates *Hondo*, as does the fact that the heroine has a son for whom the hero becomes the first of many L'Amour surrogate fathers.

The marshal's ineptitude causes the hero to take the law into his own hands, a frequent occurrence in L'Amour's writing. In addition, when Rafe Collins, an honest lawman from El Paso, confronts Matt and tries to arrest him, Matt's courteous solidity dissuades Rafe, an action echoed in later works. The hero's hiring of Pepito anticipates L'Amour's admirable absence of racial prejudice.[1]

One characteristic of early L'Amour heroes, happily absent from most later ones, is a crazed fighting lust. It boils up in Matt here, as it did in several heroes of earlier stories reprinted in *Night over the Solomons* and *West from Singapore* and as it will subsequently in Utah Blaine, Kilkenny, and most Sacketts. In between, to be sure, several heroes are more temperate. Late-appearing Joseph Makatozi (in *Last of the Breed*), however, goes as berserk as any of the earlier characters.

Gothic fictions as they are, western novels often feature lots of hidden documents. "Ride, You Tonto Raiders!" is no exception. After the final fight, in which the villain suffers a broken nose—a tedious feature in ex-pugilist L'Amour's stories—Matt finds documents to validate Jenny's land claim. But for the supreme example, see *The Broken Gun*, which starts with one document stuffed in a gun barrel and ends with the exhumation of another.

As for stylistic features, the hero of "Ride, You Tonto Raiders!" uses eyes, patience, thought-filled silence, hunches, and mayhem against villains considerably timing their one-on-one confrontations with said hero—to reach the goal of peace at the hearth. Key words in L'Amour—all used repeatedly in "Ride, You Tonto Raiders!"—include *alone, eye, home, intuition, patience, shoulder, silence, violence,* and especially *trouble* (L'Amour's favorite two-syllable word). Also employed here is typical L'Amour false foreshadowing. For example, the hero promises to drift on but instead stays put. Here, as elsewhere, L'Amour throws too many names at the reader: in less than a full page six towns-people important in the plot are named, with one not mentioned again for more than 20 pages. Place names are also fired in rapid succession: in one paragraph the reader follows the hero up Shirt Tail Creek, across Bloody Basin and Skeleton Ridge, to the Verde River, near Hardscrabble Creek. L'Amour characteristically dates his action here by indirection: it is gratuitously noted that Matt once ordered John Wesley Hardin (who flourished with guns ca. 1871–78) out of Mobeetie, and that Major [George M.] Randall surprised some Apaches near Turtle Butte a few years earlier (i.e., March 1873). L'Amour counterpoints his action with close-up scenes and panoramic summary, with habitual changes in narrative point of view.

Stylistic errors endemically mar L'Amour's prose from the start to the finish of his career. Notable in this 1949 story are his use of pronouns without identifiable antecedents, his incorrect use of "due to" as an adverbial phrase and "less" instead of "fewer," his violations of rules of parallelism, his use of awkward "that" clauses as sentence openers, his incorrect grammar (such as, "There's two"), and his quarts of clichés.

On to *Hondo*

Next is a journey through L'Amour's numerous works, touching on each but concentrating on the best, to show how he achieved a certain kind of versatility by introducing new elements in his stories over the years.

L'Amour's first novel was not *Hondo*, although it was so designated both by the author and in Bantam publicity well into the 1980s. Only with the posthumously released *Education of a Wandering Man* did L'Amour come clean: "The first novel I had published appeared in England and was called *Westward the Tide*" (136). It was released in 1950 and was not easily available in the United States until L'Amour sold the rights to Bantam in 1977.

The reason for this secrecy and dishonesty is unclear. *Westward the Tide* is rousing and suspenseful. Its hero is Mathieu Bardoul—another Matt—a former army officer and survivor of the famous Wagon Box Fight (August 1867). A decade later, he joins a wagon train of inept families heading for Black Hills gold, doing so mainly because he likes wagoner Brian Coyle and his daughter, Jaquine. Villains led by Clive Massey and supported by cowardly ex–army officer Orvis Pearson plan to massacre and pillage the wagoners and seek gold in the hills at their ease. L'Amour weaves in suspense by having a few good people in the wagons mistrust Matt, who is bad-mouthed by Massey and Pearson. L'Amour provides subplots galore: man shadows train with wagon of his own and a wanted person of initially unrevealed gender; member of good faction is along to locate brother's murderer; etc.

The historical background is well sketched. The reader is treated to sights of Deadwood and real-life Jack Langrishe's show at his Gem Theatre there and even bumps into Calamity Jane. Portugee Phillips, real-life western hero of the 230-mile winter horseback ride from Fort

Phil Kearny to Fort Laramie after the Fetterman Massacre (December 1866), gives Jaquine a favorable character reference concerning good-buddy Matt. L'Amour also pauses to present minilectures on George Armstrong Custer, Black Hills gold, the Sioux, Indian statesmanship and reverence for the land, mountain men, buffalo, European economic hardship vs. the American pioneering spirit, and western gunmen. He also offers two unwarranted cracks concerning higher education and teachers.[2]

The hero is macho enough here, as elsewhere in L'Amour's works. Matt is shot in the shoulder, side, and head (he removes the bullet from his own skull) and stabbed. As frequently happens in L'Amour's stories, the wounded hero becomes separated from help and wanders horseless over hostile terrain. In what becomes a formula, L'Amour escalates the violence in which his hero is involved. In chapter 3, Matt slaps an assailant. In chapter 9 Matt engages another adversary in fisticuffs and breaks his nose. In chapter 12 Matt taunts the main villain into a gunfight. All wandering, punching, and shooting consummated, hero and heroine are free to make a home together, with a real and symbolic hearth fire. Embracing Jaquine, Matt in a typically snappy L'Amour closure predicts that she will become a good ranch wife and puts in his order for 15 children.

Westward the Tide is unusual for being diagrammatically structured into neat quarters of three chapters each. But it is weakened when a few plot hints—stolen ammunition, telltale scars—are not followed up. And why do 15 of the characters have names beginning with *B*?

Next came *Showdown at Yellow Butte* (1953), popular, hasty, and a bit thin. In his introduction to the Gregg Press reprint (1980), Scott R. McMillan tries to show that it goes beyond the formula, avoids the faults of later amoral adult westerns, and is both romantic as to faith in the west and realistic in its use of detail. He also praises the array of minor characters in the novel, the hero of which brings lessons from a varied past to his fight against greedy Easterners eager to dispossess land-respecting ranchers. This is L'Amour's first range-war novel and is followed by about 20 more with ever-increasing artistry.

Finally, *Hondo* arrived on the scene (1953). It is a remarkable novel and deserves its status as a classic. One of its strengths is its clean and simple plot. Hondo Lane is a scout and dispatch rider for General George Crook (Arizona, 1874). Hondo aids a ranch woman named Angie Lowe and her six-year-old son, Johnny,[3] who are often deserted by worthless husband and father Ed. Hondo saves Ed but later has to kill him when the foolish fellow turns murderous. Hondo is captured by Apaches under Vittoro and is tortured, but Angie saves him by falsely identifying him as her long-gone husband. Hondo duels with Silva, a vicious Apache rival for Angie's hand. In the background is the U.S. Army, that symbol of relentlessly advancing white "civilization."

Michael T. Marsden notes that *Hondo* follows the "culturally determined pattern" of "formula fiction," but rises above the formulaic "by contributing innovative elements to an always changing and evolving story form." He then suggests that Hondo mediates between the progressive white world and the Apaches' world, epitomized by Vittoro, the aging chief. It should be added that L'Amour mediates between both twentieth-century western wildness and the conservative American fictional form, on the one hand, and twentieth-century readers, on the other. When Marsden opines that Ed Lowe is doomed because he is a hindrance to white civilization, it must be added that Hondo is no more civilized than Silva—or even Vittoro. The tragedy is not that one human side lost but that nature lost, and L'Amour knew this to be true. Apacheria has not been so much conquered as simply ruined. Marsden is on safer ground when he reasons that Hondo is the ranging male principle and Angie the ranching, domestic female principle, and when he further states that the "omega point," their staying point, "is clearly hearth and home, the end of all westward movement."[4]

We have seesaw balances in *Hondo*. The army is bungling but has brave men in it. The Apaches include good Vittoro and evil Silva. Hondo tells his new white woman about his former redskin squaw. He tells Angie that Apaches never lie and that a loving Apache couple simply vow to each other *verlebena* (meaning "forever"). (Yet they practiced polygamy and condoned wife beating.) Angie saves Hondo by a flat lie, and he lies when he tells her that her husband died bravely. Hondo undertakes to educate Johnny by letting the dog Sam snap at the boy and by taking him into the Apache territory of the desert, which is murderously arid and yet occasionally experiences rain in torrents.

More Formularies

Utah Blaine (1954) is a retrogression on L'Amour's part, being standard gory formulary fiction. Wayne C. Lee can praise it only for its smooth plot, smart hero, varied villains, and painterly sets.[5] Utah

Blaine rescues an old man from land-greedy villains, inherits a ranch from him when he is murdered later, fights for his new turf, prefers a brave female homesteader to a neighbor's spoiled daughter, regenerates a ruffian by the violence of beating him and then giving him a job, and is aided by an observant newspaperman. These western stereotypes notwithstanding, *Utah Blaine* is embarrassingly readable: it has healthy outdoor mayhem throughout and a Hollywood-style distribution of rewards at the end.

In 1954 along came *Kilkenny.* Although in its story line it is the last of a trilogy concerning a legendary gunman who helps others, it was the first to be published. The others are *The Rider of Lost Creek* (1976) and *The Mountain Valley War* (1978). In 1980 L'Amour explained that these three novels "were published in such a way that the first *book* to appear was the last one to be written, and the first and second books were published later. It is confusing [he adds] but things sometimes happen that way."[6] In 1986 he clarified matters as follows: "'A Man Called Trent' became *The Mountain Valley War* and is the second in a trilogy of stories about Lance Kilkenny."[7] Fawcett published *Kilkenny,* but Bantam issued the other two. The hero (also called Trent and Lance) is not really a loner, but he appears so as L'Amour moves him from episode to episode with only two friends to link the events. They are gorgeous Nita Riordan and her half-breed bodyguard Jaime Brigo. *Kilkenny* is the earliest L'Amour novel in which the hero does not marry the heroine by book's end. In the pulp story entitled "A Gun for Kilkenny" (in *Dutchman's Flat*), Kilkenny again leaves the heroine adoring but unwed.

The Kilkenny trilogy does not show L'Amour varying much from his formulaic pattern. Its hero is more adept with guns and fists than Bardoul or Hondo. Nineteen killings make quite a splash in *Kilkenny,* which also includes a foolish lawman, by now a common ingredient. At the end of *The Rider of Lost Creek,* the hero, wounded four times but nursed by Nita to mythic fitness, avoids marriage because he must quest away. Such an open ending is inevitable, given his creator's desire to have him become a western legend. By the time of *The Mountain Valley War,* Kilkenny is patriarchal though still young: at one point he arms a foster son by ceremonially presenting him with a Sharps rifle; at another, he gives away the lad's sister to a deserving neighbor man. By this time L'Amour was surrendering to late-1970s taste: he places much of the violence offstage, including an ambush, a suicide, and the wrecking of the villain's saloon by out-of-town miners.

The hero of *Crossfire Trail* (original version, "The Trail to Crazy Man," reprinted in *The Trail to Crazy Man*) is the first of L'Amour's several ex-sailor cowboys. Finer ones came later, but none more courageous and versatile than Rafe Caradec here. As one critic has observed, Rafe is a hero of mythic dimensions.[8] While at sea, he promised a dying shipmate that he would go to Painted Rock, Wyoming, and save the family ranch for the man's widow and daughter there. Rafe commits justifiable mutiny, gets ashore in California, persuades the heroine of his probity, and defends himself against her villainous fiancé, corrupt town officials, and a handful of anti-Custer Sioux.

A Long Plateau

By the mid-1950s L'Amour hit a plateau. His next five novels are undistinguished and do not add appreciably new features to the aging formula.

Heller with a Gun (1955) may have inspired a dramaturgically authentic movie (*Heller in Pink Tights*), but it is a weak novel. It is important in the evolution of L'Amour only because in it he first presents actors and actresses traveling and performing in the Far West. Later he will characterize such thespians more skillfully in *Reilly's Luck* and *Comstock Lode*. The *Heller* hero resembles the main man in *Showdown at Yellow Butte*: here King Mabry also declines an unsavory job, switches sides, and is hunted by his replacement. And here, as in *Utah Blaine,* are two good women, the better of whom chooses the hero in the end. Teenage Dodie Saxon, a sexy, west-toughened dancer, bides her time until Janice Ryan, a woman from Virginia, dumps Mabry because she cannot stomach the violence he employed to save her life. The first half of *Heller with a Gun* is well plotted and has good dialogue; after that, however, everything weakens, as the troupe winds its meandering way from Nebraska Territory to Virginia City.

Rye Tyler, the hero of *To Tame a Land* (1955), loses his father when the two are abandoned while wagoning west and are then attacked by Indians. The lad is aided by Logan Pollard, who as surrogate father teaches him not only to be violent but also to read. He studies Plutarch, no less. Rye's adolescence is too hastily sketched, and after that he becomes a plutocratic cattleman too quickly. Unexciting love for a girl and an exciting sequence of 10 killings by Rye culminate in his shooting Pollard, who under another name has become Rye's rival for the girl's hand. *To Tame a Land* is well paced through changes of locale

and is notable for several fine friendships among the characters. But it
is spoiled by demeaning portrayals of women and by Rye's irrelevant
decision to settle in Virginia.

Guns of the Timberlands (1955) contains more ingenious plotting but
is significant in L'Amour's development only through its well-drama-
tized rivalry between the hero, who wants to preserve good land for
grazing through scientific handling of adjacent timber, and the villain,
who does not mind upsetting the ecological balance by logging off
the trees for quick profit. The Eastern-miseducated heroine, whom
L'Amour engages to the villain to delay more heroic romancing, is
reprogrammed by western forces in due time. The cast of characters
proves too extensive for L'Amour to handle through direct action; accordingly, some drop out or leave when ordered out.

The Burning Hills (1956) is a revenge story. Trace Jordan, the hero,
must take the law into his own hands when the son of an influential
rancher kills Trace's partner. A new element is Hispanic heroine Maria
Cristina Chavero, who provides credible love interest but also, through
prejudice against gringos, less credible suspense. L'Amour makes this
five-chapter novel more complex by cleverly jump-starting it in the
middle of things, then reversing gears in a flashback to explain why
Trace is now being pursued by trackers across the burning lava of Texas
Flat.

Silver Canyon (1956; original version, "Riders of the Dawn," reprinted in *The Trail to Crazy Man*) is a mishmash of L'Amour's best
effects. It has virtually everything: hero strong but tired of just passing
through, reluctant heroine to whom hero promises marriage at first
sight[9] and offers to sire six sons, heroine's father embroiled in range
war, villain with bad army background, good old rancher who wills
spread to helpful hero and then gets killed off, spineless sheriff,
crooked lawyer in town, evidence planted against hero, silver lode
awaiting discovery, and skillful vectoring of enemy plot lines. All this
is thrilling, yes, but almost nothing is new—except for some unusual
scenery and neatly poetic prose.

Two Hits and a Miss

With *Last Stand at Papago Wells* L'Amour made a step forward. Then
followed *The Tall Stranger,* tall enough but weak. Next came *Sitka,* one
of his best. All three were published in 1957.

Last Stand at Papago Wells is a beautifully constructed narrative about

10 units of people, alone or in small groups, converging on an Arizona desert hellhole called Papago Wells. The hero Logan Cates is heading west to it. An eloping couple, Grant Kimbrough and Jennifer Fair, stop there on their intended way to Yuma. Jennifer's father, Jim Fair, and his crew pursue the pair to Papago Wells. A lone survivor of a white party butchered by Apaches escapes to it, as does a teenager named Junie, who evades her six Indian captors. They in turn are dogging her tracks. Churupati and his 21 rogue Apache-Yaquis approach Papago Wells in search of spoils, then circle it to attack. A hunter named Jim Beaupre and an anti-Apache Pima named Tony Lugo, who earlier were forced into deadly gunplay in Yuma, also arrive in Papago Wells. The remnants of a posse pursue Beaupre and Lugo there. Finally, Big Maria gallops in from Tucson, laden with heavy saddlebags.

All of this in the first 6 chapters. In the last 10 the Apaches close in, while the little crowd in their sandy sanctuary argue about leadership, strategy, desertion, and whether Big Maria has gold in her saddlebags. Punctuating this suspenseful tale of a shiplike oasis of desert fools and wise ones—all threatened by Churupati, whom the reader never sees—is death after death. L'Amour's sense of pace is exhilarating, and his story flashes with excellent touches. But it should be noted that in *Last Stand at Papago Wells* the hero is reported orphaned because "his parents died of cholera when he was fourteen," whereas it is later recorded that the hero "was sixteen at the time" his father was shot to death.[10]

The Tall Stranger is another wagons-west story. It repeats aspects of *Westward the Tide,* starts in the middle of things (à la *The Burning Hills*), and is altogether L'Amour's weakest novel to its date. Characters are badly introduced and then herded offstage for late recall; only villains die of their wounds (à la Ponga Jim Mayo yarns), while several good men survive theirs; and the romance elements are hackneyed.

Then L'Amour stepped out of the morass of formulaic fiction with *Sitka,* his first romantic historical reconstruction. Its donnée is the intrigue surrounding the Alaska Purchase. *Sitka* is half again as long as the average length of his first 13 novels, epic by comparison, and sweeping too, with a bold new look. It exemplifies L'Amour's most extensive use up to 1957 of history, which appears here not only in the background but often in the foreground as well. The hero, Jean LaBarge, is a friend of real-life Robert J. Walker (1801–1869), who was a Pennsylvania lawyer, then a U.S. senator from Mississippi, secretary of the treasury, and a financial wizard. Rob Walker was active behind the scenes with Secretary of State William H. Seward, senators Charles Sumner, William P. Fessenden, and William H. Stewart, and especially Russian Ambassador Edouard de Stoeckl—upon all of whom, and more, LaBarge dances fictional attendance in various steps. LaBarge is L'Amour's most complete hero until Mathurin Kerbouchard in *The Walking Drum*. As a youngster along the Susquehanna River, LaBarge forages without parents, since his mother is dead and his father, Smoke LaBarge, has drifted west. Jean follows later, gets to Independence, Missouri, and then travels far beyond, becoming seasoned by experience: he traps, reads Plutarch, Homer, and the Bible, is captured by Ute Indians, hears about Alaska from famed Choteau (Auguste Pierre Chouteau, 1786–1838) in St. Louis, and is shanghaied to China. Behold the hero at age 21: "Jean LaBarge looked what he was, a man born to the wild places and the tall winds. The mountain years had shaped him for strength and molded him for trial, the desert had dried him out, and the sea had made him thoughtful. His boyhood in the Great Swamp near the Susquehanna had given promise of the man he had become."[11] He takes his own schooner out of San Francisco and illegally delivers wheat to hungry Sitka, thus tangling with antagonistic Russians, both those in government office and others involved in commercial crime.

Now how can L'Amour present this swashbuckling specimen of masculinity in adventurous episodes and yet include a love interest who will not tease him into settling too quickly for hearth fire, home, and children? Easy. The author makes Jean fall in love with a Russian beauty named Princess Helena de Gagarin, now the wife of decent, lovable Russian Count Alexander Rotcheff, 30 years their elder. This diplomat, now in San Francisco, is the enemy of Baron Paul Zinnovy, the corrupt, depraved, power-thirsty villain of *Sitka*.

This novel is the best-structured of any by L'Amour to its date. Its 36 chapters fall into nine parts, including three units of a chapter each (chapters 5, 21, and 33). In the first third, Jean is presented as a lad, who then goes west, meets the three Russians, and gets his schooner. In the second third, he eludes his enemies, goes to Sitka, lets time pass, admires lovely Helena, and is forced by circumstances (including Zinnovy's shooting of old Rotcheff) to escape with her to St. Petersburg, which is rendered with much verisimilitude. The final third is crowded: an affray between LaBarge and a Russian duellist; LaBarge's audience with Helena's uncle, Czar Alexander II; the hero's return to Washington, D.C., to lobby for Alaska; and finally a sequence of rushed panels—the destruction of Jean's ship, his stints in a Siberian prison and then as a convict laborer back in Sitka, and then—but why reveal the grand operatic finale?[12]

Sitka has many virtues but also a few weaknesses. Zinnovy does not finish Rotcheff off. Helena does not inform Jean about her husband's fate for almost a year. Zinnovy sends Jean to Siberia but never assures himself of his victim's ultimate fate. Misleading foreshadowing disappoints the reader. Jean seeks his father, Smoke, but never finds him. A helpful Sitka girl kisses Jean with memorable energy but then disappears like smoke. In fact, several of Jean's friends are introduced, sketched with brief strokes, then dropped like rejected drawings. The gravest omission is of that titanic event, the Civil War, which goes virtually unmentioned, as does Abraham Lincoln.

Just before *The Daybreakers*

L'Amour published three so-so novels in 1959, a year before issuing *The Daybreakers,* his first Sackett volume. The three are *Radigan, The First Fast Draw,* and *Taggart.*

Tom Radigan of *Radigan* is another honest homesteader trying to get along just outside another dishonest town. L'Amour rings changes on the old formula, first by making the land grabber a corrupt woman backed by a fraudulent claim and a crooked crew, second by offering as a love interest young Gretchen, the adopted white daughter of Radigan's half-breed Delaware sidekick. Worth noting in this novel are the scenes in which Gretchen shoves a burning stick into the mouth of an ugly-talking heavy, unwittingly lures another bad man to his death when he happens to smell the pie she is baking for her hero, and dresses in white for the hero's climactic homecoming.

The First Fast Draw purports to parallel the life of Texas gunman Cullen Montgomery Baker (1835–69). If L'Amour had not pretended that he was writing fictionalized biography, the novel would be simply another formulaic western. The orphaned hero emerges from the Civil War having ridden with William Clarke Quantrill (1837–65), returns home to northeastern Texas hoping to farm, and falls in love with widowed Katy Thorne. Then things go against Cullen: neighborhood toughs pommel him; Thomas Warren (in real life, Thomas Orr), weird schoolteacher out of New England, woos Katie; Governor Edmund J. Davis's harsh rule turns several anti-Reconstructionists into postbellum guerrillas. These diehards include Ben Bickerstaff, Matt Kirby, Bob Lee, Bill Longley, and especially their pal Cullen.

So far so good. But L'Amour brings in so many real-life names and refers to so many real-life postbellum activities in Texas that unwary readers may wrongly conclude that *The First Fast Draw* is an accurate historical reconstruction, which it is not. L'Amour ignores Baker's first marriage, daughter, wife's death, second marriage, second wife's death, and acts of violence against freed blacks in Texas and green Union troops there. Instead of having Baker shot to death with Kirby on 6 January 1869 by the schoolteacher and his colleagues—as history records—L'Amour has him escape by a clumsy stratagem and go west with a loyal friend and their girlfriends—to marry, study law, raise horses, and remember the old days beside the Sulphur River and Lake Caddo. Thus, the theme of this novel is friendship, a commodity that the real Cullen Baker did not greatly value.

L'Amour does little service to history with *The First Fast Draw*. If he had researched Baker's life in depth, he would have learned that Bill Longley was a more feared gunslinger than Baker and that it was not Baker but Longley (1851–78) who was hanged for murder but who legend said survived.[13] Remaining enamored of Baker, L'Amour mentions him again in *Flint, Mustang Man, The Man from Skibbereen,* and *Bowdrie's Law,* and he brings him briefly into the action of *Lando.*

Taggart grew out of L'Amour's story "Trap of Gold," in which a miner digs gold out from under a huge, dangerously teetering rock. The novel adds elements from *The Burning Hills* (interracial marriage) and *Last Stand at Papago Wells* (sandstorm, confluence of groups at a dangerous desert spot in Apache territory). But there are new features as well. Instead of fighting for land, the characters are vying for gold, about which Spanish legends have long swirled. A bounty hunter pursues the justifiably homicidal hero but soon prefers the gold and the girl. The best element here is mystical "love at first sound," aroused in the active hero and the patient heroine simultaneously, when the two romantically meet and poetically speak in the starlit desert darkness.

After *Taggart* came L'Amour's eighteenth novel. It is *The Daybreakers,* and it introduced his ever-expanding readership to the famous Sackett dynasty. Since his whole Sackett saga is one big artistic unit, rather like a huge hacienda mural, it is treated, together with his Chantry and Talon books, in a later chapter—on family novels—after a consideration of his other novels. Even as L'Amour wrote his family serials, he was continuing to produce separate one-volume formulaic and romantic historical reconstructions.

Chapter Four
L'Amour at High Noon

The Daybreakers (1960), L'Amour's first Sackett novel, concerns brothers Tyrel and Orrin Sackett in 1866–67.[1] It is not the beginning, however, of the Sackett story. The novel about the establishment of the New World Sackett dynasty is *Sackett's Land* (1974), which opens in Elizabethan England in 1599 and features Barnabas Sackett. But Sackett chronological matters, as well as those generated by L'Amour's Chantry and Talon family serials, may be left to a later, separate chapter to make it possible to continue moving now through his other productions, stressing innovations and downplaying those novels that repeat formulaic clichés and special effects.

Two Aces

Next came the superb *Flint* (1960), followed by two more Sackett novels—*Sackett* (1961) and *Lando* (1962)—and then the intriguing *Shalako* (1962).

L'Amour's *Flint* was voted one of the 25 best westerns of all time by the Western Writers of America in 1977—along with L'Amour's *Hondo*. Rather like *Silver Canyon, Flint* is a collage of L'Amour's previous plot and character devices; but it also contains a few new tricks. A New Mexican gunman named Flint befriends and guides an orphan named James T. Kettleman, but then gets shot by a band of men, some of whom the kid kills. The others he remembers. Years pass, and Jim, now a rich New York businessman, leaves his vicious wife Lottie and returns to Flint's malpais hideout to die of what has been diagnosed as incurable cancer. But Kettleman steps into the middle of a three-sided fight involving land-grabbing railroad magnate Porter Baldwin, cattleman Thomas S. Nugent, and rancher Nancy Kerrigan. Further complicating this tangle are a killer named Buckdun in Baldwin's pay, a man named Gaddis who helped shoot Flint long ago and who is now Nancy's ranch hand, the arrival of Lottie, and a second opinion by a western doctor concerning the hero's alleged cancer. Meanwhile, thugs—bad and reformed—wonder if Kettleman, who has begun to call himself Flint, is the old shot-up gunman or that young kid grown up and bent on revenge.

Flint is unified by its setting and a non-human character, namely a red stallion. The novel opens with Flint dropping off a train into the woolly west. The malpais region, well rendered early, becomes the final scene for the villain, who falls onto its jagged outcroppings late in the novel. In between, to be sure, L'Amour in his customary haste leaves a few loose ends involving several of his crowded gallery of 35 named characters. A bodyguard for Nancy drops out of sight. One cowboy never justifies his billing as a dangerous gunslinger. Flint neglects to read his forwarded mail until doing so becomes dramatic. A woman is named, is criticized for being a gossip, but remains unseen. Nancy never learns the truth about Flint's "cancer." However, balancing these slips are many exemplary touches. Flint savors life in the west just when death seems imminent. The contrast between Nancy and Lottie is almost musically developed. Baldwin's respect for Flint's pugilistic prowess is stunning. Nature, embodied by the beautiful horse, the treacherous malpais, and violent rain, is wondrously painted. And the whole plot coils like a serpent.

After *Sackett* and *Lando* came *Shalako,* which introduces a new element into L'Amour's panorama of the west. Enter a daintily equipped party of more than 20 pampered European and American hunters. They include Baron General Frederick Von Hallstatt (Franco-Prussian War veteran), Hans Kreuger (Von Hallstatt's underling), Mako (his European chef), Count Henri (experienced soldier and hence Von Hallstatt's French counterpart), Charles Dagget (American diplomat), Roy Harding (Ohio orphan), western hunting-party employees displaying traits ranging from loyalty to turpitude, and four women. They are: Dagget's timorous wife, Edna; Laura David (an American senator's daughter); their flirtatious friend, Julia Page; and sensuous Lady Irina Carnarvon of Wales.[2]

Shalako, Von Hallstatt, and Irina are three of the four most important characters in this novel. The fourth is Tats-ah-das-ay-go, the "Quick Killer," a feared Apache assassin of legendary fame. The army sends units to aid the harassed whites; but the Quick Killer is superior, as are the massed Apaches on his side, to all adversaries until . . . who else? Shalako.

Now 35, Shalako was born in California; he grew up on the polyglot Texas frontier (and hence knows French and German, as well as English); he fought in the Civil War as a Union cavalry officer; and he went abroad to fight alongside the Boers in the Basuto War, then under Shir Ali in Afghanistan, and then under Comte MacMahon from Metz to Bazaine during the Franco-Prussian War. Next Shalako idled a while in postwar Paris (meeting Edouard Manet, Edgar Degas, and Emile Zola); and lately he has been drifting in America's Southwest as free as Zuni winds. He lectures the camp on a dozen of L'Amour's favorite topics: nature's wonders, Indians, horses, women, and military tactics, which he learned not only the hard way but also from such obscure authorities as Vegetius, Saxe, and Jomini, whom he impresses the European soldiers by naming.[3] Shalako ridicules Von Hallstatt for bringing ladies on a dangerous expedition, for being rank-conscious, and for insanely hoping for "a little brush with" the Apaches (12).

Among the virtues of *Shalako* are its combat scenes, character-defining responses of various individuals to danger, and Lady Irina's love for Shalako. But the novel is hard to read, because each of its four chapters is too long and too packed, each chapter has awkward shifts in narrative point of view, and there are too many characters. L'Amour substitutes here, as elsewhere, narrative complexity and confusion for more profound character and incident development. Two high points in *Shalako* are Irina's gift to the hero of a noble Arabian steed and the hero's respect for his final adversary, Tats-ah-das-ay-go, whom he declares, "almost in anguish, in admiration: 'Warrior! Brother!'" (167).

A Low Octave

L'Amour's next eight novels show little innovation. Apart from *How the West Was Won* (1963), each is short.

Killoe (1962) is a simple cattle-drive story. It avoids routine status by two deviations in the formula. First the hero has an unstable foster brother who captures the affections of said hero's naughty girlfriend, and then the father of the hero turns over leadership of the drive to him. The novel includes effective scenes of dust eating along the April 1858 trail from Texas to New Mexico and memorable descriptions of desert sounds. But *Killoe* is not recommended for mature audiences.

Nor is *High Lonesome* (1962), which tries to generate reader sympathy for a prankster-robber who in self-revulsion seeks to shed the vestigial remains of his past once he meets a lithe girl and her time-gentled father, himself a wild fellow in his youth. But L'Amour should never have expected even his most loyal readers to forgive a "hero" who plans a bank robbery that his cohorts later carry out. It is even revealed that long ago the "hero" was felonious south of the border; but that was in another country—and, besides, the Mexican is dead.

Fallon (1963) has to be L'Amour's poorest novel, with *The Tall Stranger* and *The Proving Trail* being almost as bad. Fallon is a card sharp, driven out of one town by a lynch mob to an improbably deserted one, which he tries to lease to merchants wagoning in with goods for sale to later suckers. Silly incidents are so unremitting in *Fallon* that it might qualify as a satire on the western novel but for the fact that satire meant nothing to L'Amour.

Next came *How the West Was Won* (1963), which, as adapted from the film script of James R. Webb, is a five-act dramatic epic. L'Amour labeled its parts "The Rivers," "The Plains," "The [Civil] War," "The Iron Horse," and "The Outlaws." Most old western buffs probably remember the movie, with its big cast of at least 18 first-rate actors and actresses. But some movie buffs, and even some literary critics, wrongly think to this day that the cinerama extravaganza followed L'Amour's book. All the same, L'Amour ably narrates the aid that fur trapper Linus Rawlings (James Stewart in the movie) gives the Prescott and Harvey families, who are in danger on the turbulent Ohio River (ca. 1840). Lilith Prescott (played by Debbie Reynolds) accepts money from Rawlings and heads west to become actress, wife, and surrogate matriarch. Her sister Eve (Carroll Baker) marries Rawlings, who does not survive Shiloh (1862), although their son Zebulon (George Peppard) does. Then, staying in the army, he too goes west for more adventures. The plot stretches across a continent and includes activities of four generations of pioneering stock. Eve, the daughter of Zebulon Prescott (Karl Malden) and his wife Rebecca (Agnes Moorehead), marries Rawlings; many years later Zebulon, one of their four children, becomes the father of Prescott, Linus, and Eve. It is likely that the nature of its multigenerational story lines inspired L'Amour to continue his Sackett series, which by 1963 numbered only 3 volumes. After all, if L'Amour from the start of his Sackett series had some 20 or more volumes in mind, then why did he name the second book to appear *Sackett*?

Abijah Catlow is the hero of *Catlow* (1963) and, like many other western outlaws in reality and in fiction, was legally innocent of wrongdoing. But an ungrateful former boss and a dishonest lawman try to frame Bijah and hang him for rustling. He escapes and aids his boyhood friend Ben Cowan, now a deputy marshal. The goofy plot—a chase for $2 million in lost Benito Juárez gold—carries good Bijah and tarnished Ben into Mexico and makes them acquainted with contrasting heroines, for romantic balance. (Each man promises to name his first son for the other.) The white heroine is faithful Cordelia; the Hispanic heroine is resourceful Rosita, who mentions quite unnecessarily that her cousin is Tyrel Sackett's wife, up in Mora, New Mexico.

In *Dark Canyon* (1963), as in many earlier novels, L'Amour again substitutes plot contortions for profundity. At one point there are eight lines of action simultaneously aimed at the hero's ranch. Young Gaylord Riley wants to quit a life of crime. So his older partners advance funds for him to start a ranch and a herd near Dark Canyon, by Fable Canyon, near the Sweet Alice Hills, beside the Painted Desert—quite a palette of colorful place names. But the newcomer is opposed by villains who are themselves rivals for the land and the heroine. In return for use of the tainted money from his former colleagues in crime, Riley has promised to offer them sanctuary if needed. Need comes, and so does Tell Sackett—for no reason except that L'Amour wanted to keep the name Sackett before his readers' eyes pending release of *Mojave Crossing, The Sackett Brand, Mustang Man,* etc. Why didn't L'Amour make something of the latent symbolism in the name Dark Canyon? After all, Riley's solid fortune is built over the dark canyons of stolen funds.

Hanging Woman Creek (1964) repeats several old plot elements—a train ride west, naive Europeans entering the harsh west, and quick land bequeathals—but adds a few new ingredients. The hero Barney "Pronto" Pike, though honest, is a loser reluctant to reform, while the catalyst speeding his self-improvement is a well-delineated black man named Eddie Holt. He becomes Pronto's partner, boxing instructor, and mentor. Pronto is caught between harmless nesters and a cattle baron with vigilante-style hired guns. Montana heroes John Xavier Beidler (1831–90) and Granville Stuart (1834–1918) are mentioned but never endowed with reality. Exciting, and new too, is a unique kind of villainess. She is a wandering, demented woman whose motivation is askew but fascinating. Why didn't L'Amour somehow relate her malady to the curious title of this novel?

Conn Dury is the overqualified hero of *Kiowa Trail* (1964). L'Amour realized that the main action of this short novel was perilously thin. It concerns the blockade of a Kansas town by cattle-driving Texans, incensed because one of their number has been murdered therein. So L'Amour includes six flashbacks out of chronological order but in a dramatic crescendo. The present situation is this: Kate Lundy, a rich

widow, owns a Texas herd and is driving it north with her 19-year-old
brother Tom as a crew member. Her trail boss is Dury. Tom violates
the curfew of the town by visiting a depraved tease who gets him killed
to enhance her reputation. So Kate leases adjacent railroad land, fences
the town in, and undertakes to destroy it by blocking commerce in
and out. Meanwhile, flashbacks reveal that Dury is a good deal like
Tarzan: orphaned by an Indian massacre, he lived among Apaches and
was later rescued by a traveling British officer named James Sotherton,
whose friendship and then murder led Dury (after incomplete revenge)
to England—to meet Sotherton's father, Sir Richard, and attend
school. Next, Dury wandered through western goldfields, became a
Texas Ranger, happened to save Kate and Tom from Apaches who
killed her husband, then after service in the Union army during the
Civil War returned to Kate as her overseer. The only functional connection between Dury's zestful past and Kate's present attempt to
throttle the Kansas town is the fact that the one surviving killer of
Sotherton is there. The flashbacks of *Kiowa Trail* are more interesting
than the main action.

Seven More

Of the next seven novels, two more concern Sacketts. They are *Mojave Crossing* (1964) and *The Sackett Brand* (1965). The other five are
The High Graders (1965), *The Key-Lock Man* (1965), *The Broken Gun*
(1966), *Kid Rodelo* (1966), and *Kilrone* (1966). *The Broken Gun* is the
best.

The High Graders stars another lark-loving criminal. Here he is an
ex-rustler who becomes so honest when associating with former cohorts
that he has to shoot a few of them. New in this novel is the killing of
a female criminal by irate miners. A charming symbolic touch is provided when filthy water from the gold mines pollutes the source of
drinking water for cattle. Moral: modern technology can ruin an age-
old natural process. L'Amour will use again this story's scariest situation: being trapped in a mine shaft.

The hero of *The Key-Lock Man* (evolved from the early story "Dutchman's Flat," reprinted in *Dutchman's Flat*) is Matt Keelock, who
though innocent of crime is pursued by a posse of six men of various
degrees of toughness and misgivings. The opening comic tone gives
way to a somber one once the heroine is introduced. European-born
and a veritable Viking, Kristina, after killing her vile lover, escaped to

America by answering an advertisement for a mail-order bride. But then she objected to the villain she delivered herself to in the so-called virgin land of the west. All of this is action antecedent to the start of the novel. Enter Mr. Keelock, who is already Kristina's nice western husband. The plot of *The Key-Lock Man,* though tightened into many knots, is quite ordinary, featuring for example, a train of wagons laden with California gold lost somewhere in the Painted Desert region of Arizona or Utah.

Then came the best of this group of books. It is *The Broken Gun,* one of L'Amour's most unusual novels to its date and the first of only three set in the twentieth century. (The others are *Last of the Breed* and *The Haunted Mesa.*) Yet it too is a western—with western hero, Hispanic helper figure, lawman, land-greedy villains, heroine in distress, vixeny villainess, urgent messages (by telephone, not smoke signals), transportation by jeep (also horse), and even neo–chuck wagon (i.e., station wagon)—all in remote stretches of southeastern Arizona. The plot jumps into action when L'Amour's most autobiographical hero, combat veteran and western writer Dan Sheridan, finds an 1870s Toomey family journal stuffed into the barrel of a broken Bisley Colt he bought about 1962. The journal leads Sheridan to investigate land fraudulently held by descendants of the killers of the Toomeys. Nothing is very new about the main elements of the plot. Villain invites hero onto his ranch and into his clutches; up-front hero boasts of his evidence and intentions, escapes trap in mountains, takes evasive action, and joins heroine; heroine is caught while hero is helped by resourceful native. Stock plot properties include fire, pusillanimous neighbors, assorted fights, tardy arrival of law, location of long-lost documents. The charm of *The Broken Gun* lies not in its story line, with its time-honored Gothic ingredients, but in L'Amour's delightful translation of those ingredients into twentieth-century terms.

For a change, *Kid Rodelo* has a simple plot. Released from Yuma prison for a gold robbery he did not commit, Rodelo joins some thugs, led by the friend who fingered him into prison as a jest, on a caper south of the border to pick up said gold. After all, the Kid did time for it. Two simplistic morals emerge from this weak novel: love of gold can corrupt a potentially bad person, and suffering can regenerate a good one who has had a bad experience.

Kilrone is L'Amour's earliest thorough treatment of military life in the West. Much of the novel is standard fare: glory-seeking commanding officers, sneaky and inept Indians; Eastern villain in the west to make money by providing the post with card games, whiskey, and women, and the Indians with whiskey and guns; payroll being wagoned in to the undermanned post; long-suffering wives restricted to base; and hero with a past so varied that he is now equal to any contingency. Much in *Kilrone* is also fresh. The hero is Barnes Kilrone, West Point graduate and former American military observer of the Franco-Prussian War. The present time is vaguely after Chief Joseph's 1877 retreat. Kilrone, now a civilian, informs the post in northern Nevada that Bannock Indians in the region have wiped out a patrol under the colonel. But acting commander Major Frank Paddock disbelieves Kilrone because when the two men were in Paris as war observers they fought over a woman named Denise de Caslou. Although Paddock married her, he feels that she pines for still-single Kilrone. This is untrue, since Denise is happy and loves the American west. Not surprisingly, she has a gorgeous female friend at the post. She is Betty Considine, niece of the post surgeon. She falls in love with Kilrone faster than in a Hollywood love story. But before he can propose to her in a way typical of L'Amour's heroes—"Ever been to California? . . . It's a nice place for a honeymoon"[4]—trouble must be saddled up, mounted, and ridden at the reader. *Kilrone* is balanced in the best formulaic western tradition (see Cawelti, 66–67). Varied scenes on base alternate with outdoor pursuits staged so that aggressive white soldiers become the redskins' quarry.

Two More Sacketts in a Seven-Pack

By the late 1960s, L'Amour had become accustomed to platooning Sacketts and non-Sacketts in winning formations. Among the next seven books come two new Sackett segments. They are *Mustang Man* (1966) and *The Sky-Liners* (1967). Each introduces a new Sackett cousin for Tell and his brothers, and both feature lost gold. Fresher in plotting are some of the five non-Sacketts, which are *Matagorda* (1967), *Down the Long Hills* (1968), *Chancy* (1968), *Brionne* (1968), and *The Empty Land* (1969).

Well-titled *Matagorda* contains L'Amour's best evocation of place until *Last of the Breed*. Its hero is Tappan "Tap" Duvarney, veteran on the Union side during the Civil War and then an Indian fighter. He wants to join forces with Tom Kittery from anti-Yankee Texas in a cattle venture. But touchy Tom, whom Tap captured during the war but befriended, prefers feuding against the Munson family to riding herd with Tap from Matagorda to Dodge City. And so do Tom's hot-blooded hands. So L'Amour's hero here steps not into a range war, as earlier heroes have done, but into a gory Southern feud. Fine innovation, so far. The author commendably complicates matters by introducing a contrasting pair of women. One is Jessica Trescott, Tap's loyal Virginia fiancée. The other is Mady Coppinger, Tom's fiancée, who is as modern in her addiction to city lights as Jessica is traditional in deferring to male authority. *Matagorda* also features a unique oddball L'Amour villain. He is pro-Munson Jackson Huddy, a backshooter but also a churchgoer and a respecter of womenfolk. *Matagorda* has a few defects. It parades brothers Lightly and Darkly Foster, in the story mainly for the humor of their names. Eight hundred cows and three cowboys get up, break camp, and depart—all while the hero sleeps through the noise. L'Amour seems too ready—as are many other traditional western writers—to regard murder as rightly forgotten once it is avenged and also to let female wrongdoers off with a mere wrist slap. One rare use of symbolic action, however, makes up for all weaknesses here. Lovely Jessica, whose appearance halfway through the novel transposes it into a new key, loses to a flood every tangible shred of her aristocratic past—family pictures, books, clothes, and the like. She is thus portrayed as giving up all her possessions to follow her man into the rugged west and a new life.[5]

Down the Long Hills is unlike anything else L'Amour ever wrote. It is unified in time, place, and action. In September 1848 seven-year-old Hardy Collins must walk west through cold Wyoming hills toward Fort Bridger and in the process must save Betty Sue Powell, his three-year-old companion. All the adults in the wagon carrying them west have been massacred by Comanches. Having been schooled in wood-craft by his widowed father, Hardy is equal to the task. But only barely, because opposing him are three enemy forces. They are an Indian who covets the boy's stallion, a bear dubbed Old Three Paws, and a pair of white thugs back from an early tour of robbery in the California goldfields. Closing in to aid Hardy, however, are his father and two mountain men. So in this narrative of pursuit, evasion, and rescue are five lines of action. Narrative unity is intensified by the unusually small number of characters—only eight. The best features of *Down the Long Hills* are Hardy's resourcefulness, the depiction of a superstitious Indian, the thugs' shades of evil, the two noble animals, and the father's confident love for his child. The story might have profited from some polyphonic variety. L'Amour's concentration on cold, hunger, fatigue, and fear is too unrelieved. Also, L'Amour should have stayed with the child's compelling point of view more than he does. He often shifts to the point of view of one or another adult, perhaps necessarily, given the plot lines. But at one point he awkwardly reports that "the Indian did not, as yet, realize that he, too, was followed."[6]

Chancy is mostly an unpleasant combination of previously used plot ingredients. In it a fatherless young drifter (as in *To Tame a Land*), who is hated by his neighbors (see *The First Fast Draw*) and who has been to sea (*Crossfire Trail, Sitka*), gains rights to a cattle herd very fast (*Killoe*) and is too happy-go-lucky for his own good (*Fallon*). A gun provides evidence (*The Broken Gun*), and the evil force is feminine (*Radigan*). And a good woman travels far to meet the hero (*Matagorda*). Though starting well, *Chancy* is marred by these familiar plot elements.

Brionne begins with a fresh situation. James Brionne, another former military man of western and European expertise, is now a reluctant statesman in Washington, D.C. He is also a husband and father. His son Mat is six. How to get these two males west? Have the lovely wife and mother assaulted at home, before the boy's very eyes and while the husband is away. She resists the villains, kills one, and commits suicide to avoid what she regards as a fate she could not live with. The other thugs and Mat separately flee. So much for the first chapter. Next, Brionne seeks revenge without success, gets away for a second chance, and hopes to give his traumatized son a new beginning in the Far West. Would one ever guess that Brionne and Mat, once they get beyond Cheyenne and Promontory, might find not only that second chance but also a second wife, a second mother, maybe even silver in the mountains, and perhaps the remnants of the gang of would-be rapists from back home? An amusing touch is Brionne's conferring in St. Louis with Ulysses S. Grant.

In *The Empty Land* L'Amour presents the early days of yet another tough town. Aptly called Confusion, it grows too fast once gold is discovered in its outskirts. A miner who made the strike thinks naively that reason and not guns can talk to and govern lawless thugs descending on the region for loot. Not so. Therefore the decent element must appeal to wearily experienced Matt Coburn, who has just happened by but is reluctant to become Confusion's lawman briefly and one of its Boot Hill occupants more permanently. L'Amour adopts a fatalistic tone here. Matt happens to rescue and have dinner with a beautiful woman who is ranching thereabouts; to hear how killers handled the former town marshal; and to help a traveling actress who stagecoaches in. So he is caged both by circumstances and by his own temperament. He cinematically straps on his guns, which he is adept at wielding. He posts a list of the 70 most unwanted men in Confusion, and by stages he expels all but a die-hard 10 percent or so whom he naturalistically kills. *The Empty Land* is memorable for the hero's reluctance to return to gunfighting, his willingness to nurture the psychological development of a few wavering young persons, the differing responses to curative violence registered by the two distinct heroines, and the quick-time march of incidents.

Sextet with Three Themes

Of the next six novels, two are Sacketts. They are *The Lonely Men* (1969), which takes Tell Sackett into Apache territory, and *Galloway* (1970), which details more adventures of two of Tell's cousins introduced in *The Sky-Liners*. The four non-Sacketts are *Conagher* (1969), *The Man Called Noon* (1970), *Reilly's Luck* (1970), and *North to the Rails* (1971). Three of them play variations on old motifs, and the fourth introduces the name Chantry to L'Amour's readers.

Conagher is a fine novel. Its titular hero is a middle-aged Civil War veteran tired of fighting and drifting and eager for a place to call home. The heroine is young Evie Teale, whose juiceless old husband's death leaves her with his two kids from a former marriage. One is a sturdy boy; the other, a snippy girl. Evie supports herself and them by running a New Mexico stagecoach station. L'Amour neatly characterizes her and several other females in what becomes a solid depiction of harsh life for lonely women in the late nineteenth-century west. Onto the scene come two more women. One is seeking her missing outlaw brother; the other is their aunt. L'Amour poignantly dramatizes the failure of their search. Another woman enters. She is a hard young thing, aboard a coach stopping only a few minutes, with some wounded men whom she tends carefully. But most gripping is Evie, who is protected by an armor of toughness that shields her undying gentleness within. In her limited free time, she traces a floral pattern on her dirt floor, to make it appear carpeted, and also writes out sentimental messages and mails them on tumbleweeds, hoping that her knight in shiny chaps will find one and come for her. Enter Conagher.

Late in *The Man Called Noon* it is reported that Easterner Jonas Mandrin, former correspondent, author, arms expert, arms-company founder and owner, hunter, and world traveler, lost his wife and child, changed his name to Ruble Noon, and hired out to Tom Davidge (now dead) to come west and kill evildoers who were squeezing his ranch. Early in the novel, however, it is reported that one of those villains has just shot Noon in the head, causing amnesia. Yes, *The Man Called Noon* employs one of the most indigestible plot ingredients. Yet it is with great subtlety that L'Amour has the past gradually emerge from the hero's inner vision as events rush his new identity through horrible crises toward a future improved not only by returning memory but also by Tom's fetching daughter Fan. *The Man Called Noon* has L'Amour's most complicated plot. It is a veritable tangle of narrative difficulties, the threads of which are impossible to summarize. Present are railroad car and cave, gangs of rival crooks, enigmatic letters, mountain cabin, escape route by shaft in mountain rocks, ambushes by ranch and saloon, midnight rendezvous in lawyer's office, greedy judge and bad woman, good Mexican stablemen, research in newspaper files, rescue of condemned Mexican husband of fine woman, avalanche, phenomenal marksmanship, escape through underground passage, treasure map, tree house, stuffed strongbox, train ride, and shootout.

By the time of *Reilly's Luck,* L'Amour had a firm grip on his narrative techniques and subject matter, as well as a devoted readership. This novel is accordingly a vivid and popular combination of old themes with new variations. Will Reilly's "luck" is his adopted boy Valentine "Val" Darrant, who as an unwanted child is marked by his unprincipled mother, Myra Cord, for murder; he is saved, however, and is nurtured, and grows up to become the hero of the story. This concentration on a youngster's training is reminiscent of earlier L'Amour fiction, but otherwise Val's upbringing is unique. Reilly is a card player, marksman, associate of shady westerners, reader, and traveler. So lucky Val learns about poker, books, fists, guns, criminals, Europe, Philadelphia, and New York. After being a teenage Texas cowboy, he rejoins Reilly, until the latter is murdered by a trio paid by Prince Pavel (a Russian gambler who would have profitably married off his cousin Princess Louise but for Reilly's intervention in Innsbruck). To pad the novel, L'Amour follows Val through several educative years—partial revenge, Mississippi River salvage work, law study in New York, and love in the west. Then L'Amour bends probability: Prince Pavel, in New York with Louise, meets Val's evil mother, Myra, widowed, rich, and doubly venomous through not only commercial ambition but also recent awareness that her son is alive. So they journey to the west to consummate dastardly machinations. Chapter 23 of *Reilly's Luck* is a masterpiece of plot-line vectoring, as nine characters prepare for battle, with the new Windsor Hotel in Denver (ca. early 1880s) as backdrop.

This sprawling novel has enough action for a prime-time TV soap. There are more than 120 characters, counting dead people whose actions bear on the plot and historical persons who could be given cameo spots (Billy the Kid, Robert Fleury, Wild Bill Hickok, James Hill, Allen Pinkerton, Joe Slade). At the one-quarter mark, Reilly is killed. At the halfway point, Val's mother hires Pinkerton the detective, and the plot takes a ponderous turn. At the three-quarters mark, the Prince and his party head west for his comeuppance. Plot lines often trail off in midchapter, and on occasion Val's point of view is awkwardly eclipsed. In fact, *Reilly's Luck* has a dozen authorial gaffes. The heroine, named Boston, says that she is spoken for but is not. Names trouble L'Amour here: Dube becomes Duke; Joe Slade becomes Jack Slade; and Pike becomes Peck, even though another character is also named Peck. A letter is delivered to the wrong post office, so that Val can pick it up there. Myra fancies that she can inherit the property of the son she abandoned. (Surely lawyer Val could file an ironclad will and cut her out.) Val rushes to marry Boston to make her his heiress, then neglects to write his will and postpones their wedding. A renowned pugilist tells Val that they should amiably mix it up, but they don't. It is stated that Val never saw Bill Hickok again, but then he does.[7]

North to the Rails is a so-so western mentioned here only because it is the first novel to be published of what was initially billed as a series of volumes devoted to L'Amour's Chantry family. It introduces Tom Chantry, the son of the titular hero of *Borden Chantry,* published half a dozen years later. This nonsequential narration of the saga only confused fans while permitting genealogically minded critics to conclude that L'Amour had been haphazardly building his "House of Chantry" when death unfortunately halted construction. Sequential storytelling, however, was never L'Amour's forte.

North to the Rails is a cattle-drive story rendered different through its hero's initial belief that he need not use guns in the reasonable west. In addition to an unprincipled villainess, the plot features a tepid "non-love" story, the heroine of which contributes nothing to the action and only poignancy to the tone. Silliest of all is Tom's betting a thug on the trail north that he can last the duration of the drive. The result is rousing but wobbly.

Chapter Five

L'Amour at Sunset

L'Amour faced the 1970s in full possession of his storytelling powers. *North to the Rails* was his fiftieth novel. By this time he had introduced his reading public to his Sackett and Chantry clans. The Talon family was also much on his mind. In addition, he was planning more formulary novels and romantic historical reconstructions.

Six More, Including Sacketts and a Chantry

L'Amour's next six novels were *Under the Sweetwater Rim* (1971), *Tucker* (1971), *Callaghen* (1972), two more Sackett segments—*Ride the Dark Trail* (1972) and *Treasure Mountain* (1972)—plus *The Ferguson Rifle* (1973), which deals with an early nineteenth-century Chantry. The narrator of *Ride the Dark Trail* is Logan Sackett, another cousin of Tell Sackett and his brothers. *Treasure Mountain* describes Tell's and Orrin's efforts to trace the final days of their missing father. *The Ferguson Rifle* is narrated by Ronan Chantry, a new Chantry, who like many earlier L'Amour heroes heads west for regeneration, and finds in the process male companionship, adventure, danger, gold, and romance.

Under the Sweetwater Rim again combines much that is familiar with a few new elements. The hero, U.S. army Lieutenant Tenadore Brian, is (as in *Shalako* and *Kilrone*) a military man with American and European experience. He and another central male figure, Reuben Kelsey, were once friends but now are on opposite sides of the law (as in *Catlow*). And in typical L'Amour fashion, Brian is shot in the skull and unhorsed but falls to safety in concealing vegetation. At the same time, the complex plot contains some refreshingly new material. Brian, on leave, is disliked by his inept commanding officer, whose reputation he saves and whose daughter he loves. Military units and regional Indian raiding parties contain both virtuous and evil men—which creates a bit of a muddle. *Under the Sweetwater Rim* has 21 jumpy chapters, with shifts in narrative point of view that are hard to follow. The action moves west from Fort Laramie toward Fort Bridger and South Pass City. Although the time is specified as April 1864, hints are carelessly included that the Civil War (which did not actually end until 1865) is over.

Tucker is an effective story of a teenage hero seeking to avenge his father's death on the cattle trail and also to recover funds advanced by Texas neighbors to finance the herd. Desire for revenge takes Shell Tucker across dangerous terrain and on to California, but more significantly to a timely awareness that violence begets violence and that revenge can ruin its seeker.

Callaghen is yet another army novel but with a slick plot twist and other clever features, all of which make it a first-rate action story. An impostor, posing as an army lieutenant ordered to a Southwestern post, enters the region with a concealed map to a river of gold. He rashly takes a command into the Mojave Desert and is killed by hostile Indians. Only then does the hero come in. He is versatile, Irish-born Mort Callaghen, with a soldier-of-fortune past that includes duty in the Middle East, Afghanistan, and China. He must find that map and thus discomfit the anti-Irish commanding officer (Major Ephraim Sykes). Callaghen must also save some patrols ordered by Sykes into the merciless desert and win the love of a heroine. One comic note: in the novel, Sykes is said to have gained his Civil War fame because he charged the enemy—when his horse ran wild. A more serious note is sounded when the hero and the heroine decide that a single-minded search for gold can be injurious to one's spiritual health.

Next came *The Ferguson Rifle*. It is another narrative about lost gold. But this novel, featuring a bookish hero, Ronan "Scholar" Chantry,[1] and set just after the Louisiana Purchase, takes on new coloration. Ronan is the earliest Chantry in respect to time of action. *The Ferguson Rifle* is loaded with hints as to his Irish family connections, to tease the reader into hoping for Chantry follow-ups. Further, the villain, Rafen Falvey, takes on mythic dimensions that help prepare the reader for later characters such as Barnabas Sackett and Tatton Chantry. The heroine is a damsel-in-distress teenager. She is attractive, to be sure; but would an eight-man party, intent on securing a fortune, give up their direct route to it so as to escort her from the Dakotas to Canada, on her way back home to Ireland? It is also strange that the titular rifle proves less useful to the hero than an old knife from India.

Three Strange Rescuers

The Man from Skibbereen (1973), *The Quick and the Dead* (1973), and *The Californios* (1974) feature three different men, each on a rescue mission. Crispin "Cris" Mayo, from Skibbereen, Ireland, gets jilted at home and migrates to America, to work on the railroad. But, abandoned by mistake out west, he overhears a conspiracy to kill some post–Civil War generals, including William Tecumseh Sherman and Philip Sheridan, who are hunting in Wyoming Territory in 1868. *The Quick and the Dead* presents a wagons-west hero who gallantly aids a good man and his fine wife. The action quickly turns unusual (for a L'Amour novel), because the hero just might fall in love with the other man's wife—while the other man is still alive. In *The Californios* a Mexican-Irish sailor returns from the sea to aid his mother, who is in danger of losing her California home. The son can rescue her only with the miraculous intervention of a very aged Hispanic friend and his ghostly Indian associates. Thus, these three novels startlingly mix old and new ingredients.

Cris Mayo is an engaging lad. Being from Ireland in the nineteenth century, he knows horses[2] and fisticuffs. But he becomes adept too fast in the use of western firearms. In spite of very recently having had a fingertip shot off, he enters a boxing contest that provides him a stake to venture on to California, to raise horses there. He has fallen under the spell of the enchanting west, which he makes the subject of this ever-timely soliloquy: "Let us not lose this, . . . let us not lose this, God, for there is no greater beauty."[3]

In *The Quick and the Dead,* Duncan McKaskel and his wife Susanna, both Easterners wagoning west about 1858 with their 12-year-old son Tom, meet up with hero Con Vallian. Once he observes that Duncan is brave and that Susanna is a good wife and mother, Con backs them all the way—but in ways that strengthen their independence. L'Amour flirted timidly at this point in his career with the possibility of more graphic sexuality and violence. A sensualist villain announces his ambition to kill both Con and Duncan, then torture and rape Susanna. L'Amour also succumbed here to the temptation to use too much violence: in the last chapter, Con shoots a secondary villain above his belt buckle and then under his right eye. Next comes the climactic violence. How to rid the homesteaders of the villain? Con must shoot him in chest, arm, leg, then somewhere more fatal three more times. L'Amour exaggerates the western code of heroic fair play when he has

Duncan, armed with a rifle at a window of his home, simply watch the one-on-one gunplay. Although L'Amour's writing is never A+ correct, *The Quick and the Dead* is especially marred by some of his most atrocious grammatical errors and publisher's typos. Thus the following: "The Huron had shot at what he believed was him"; "he cralwed for . . . yards"; "'womens fixin'"; "rising bodly up"; "no one [was] sure of he who rode beside him"; and "searching for Vallian, whom he knew was somewhere near."[4]

The Californios is one of L'Amour's most unusual novels to its date. The hero is Sean Mulkerin, 22-year-old son of Eileen Mulkerin (formerly of Ireland) and deceased Jaime Mulkerin (formerly of the Mexican army). Their other son is a monk named Michael, who can use a rifle all right but prefers to pray. Sean would seem to need more than prayers to help their mother keep her Malibu ranch from land grabbers in 1844. To add to his gallery of enemies, L'Amour has Sean, now in Acapulco, rescue Mariana de la Cruz from evil Andres Machado, her fiery fiancé, whom she never wanted. Sean then sets sail for California to try to bail out his mother by selling furs, but he knows that he has too little cargo to make the money she needs. Ultimately Sean is aided by the centegenarian Juan, his mystical surrogate father, and Juan's nonmaterial Indian helpers, whose sandals whisper tracklessly in the sand and back and forth across time itself. A beautiful touch is L'Amour's making a symbol for the time barrier out of heat waves rising from the desert.

Six, Mostly in Extenuation

Of the next six novels, three add details to the ongoing Sackett series, one is the first Talon novel, one is another Chantry installment, and one adds to the legend of Kilkenny.

Providing more Sackett information are *Sackett's Land* (1974), which introduces dynasty founder Barnabas Sackett; *The Man from the Broken Hills* (1975), incorrectly billed by both the author and his publisher as a Sackett volume from the date of its publication until 1988, when they first correctly identified it as a Talon story (*Companion*, 245); and *To the Far Blue Mountains* (1976), a beautifully titled continuation of Barnabas's New World adventures. *Rivers West* (1975) tells how Jean Daniel Talon leaves the Gaspé Peninsula to trek southwest and west, building and exploring as he advances from Maine to Pittsburgh to St. Louis, and beyond. *Over on the Dry Side* (1975) grafts an account of a widower and his son, as they homestead in Colorado, onto the story of Owen Chantry's arrival at their site—really his house and land—for the purpose of finding a family treasure hidden thereabouts. *The Rider of Lost Creek* (1976) continues the story of Kilkenny, here summoned to Texas to break up a ranch war between the Lords and the Steeles, whose squabble is caused by neither faction but rather by an Eastern villain eager to pick up the pieces, which could include Nita Riordan, Kilkenny's undying but unsatisfied love.

Rivers West is a supermelodramatic period study. It turns on the scheme of a villain to seize the Louisiana Purchase. The villain needs the heroine because of her deceased father's network of merchant spies. The heroine could use the strength and resourcefulness of hero Talon but instead acts class-consciously toward him because he is a ship-builder (i.e., a mere laborer). Narrator Jean Talon is strong enough; he records that "the bulges of my deltoids were like melons."[5] Shrewd too, he senses that Tabitha Majoribanks—that is the heroine's high-class name—should be just about right to help him generate a mighty brood. Detailed commentary about earlier Talons is designed to whet readers' curiosity, much of which L'Amour's death has left unsatisfied.

Then came *The Man from the Broken Hills*. To the novice reader, it is merely another complex western involving twins and mistaken identity, though it also realistically depicts cowboys at their hard work on the range, rather than at their hard play in saloons and elsewhere. However, this novel must be adverted to later because Milo's mother Emily was a Sackett before marrying Reed Talon. Hence Milo, their son, is doubly important in any consideration of L'Amour's Sackett and Talon family sagas.[6]

Over on the Dry Side hangs in time awkwardly between the early action of *The Ferguson Rifle* and later events in *Borden Chantry* and *North to the Rails*. The relationship of Owen Chantry to other Chantry family members, however, is unfortunately not specified here. Nor did help come with *Fair Blows the Wind,* published still later but reaching back in time to introduce family progenitor Tatton Chantry. As these books attest, L'Amour specialized in confusing and teasing his fans. The primary narrator of *Over on the Dry Side* is teenager Doban ("Doby") Kernohan, who with his lonely Pa finds the body of Clive Chantry. They bury him, take over his spread as squatters, but then must welcome Clive's scholarly brother Owen, who is also very awkwardly included as a part-time narrator. Owen permits the two Kernohans to stay as tenants working on shares, and he proves to be adept not only as a storyteller but also as a fighter. Furthermore, he catches the eye of an attractive female neighbor, which upsets Doby, to the delight of the reader. The girl turns out to be the stepdaughter of the leader of assorted heavies, all milling about because rumor has it that Clive brought back a treasure from Mexico. Thinking it gold, they can never believe that a historical manuscript could be worth more than tangible riches. A fine literary feature here is the use of Tennyson's majestic "Ulysses," one of L'Amour's touchstone poems, as the source of clues leading to the treasure. An interesting element of the narrative is the steady peeling away of members of the gang, until only its hard core of evil remains.

Two Winners between Two Losers

Next came *Where the Long Grass Blows* (1976), *Borden Chantry* (1977), *Fair Blows the Wind* (1978), and *The Mountain Valley War* (1978). The first and last are only minimally competent, but the middle two are generally well composed.

Where the Long Grass Blows tells about a cowboy entering a strange region to stake his claim. At first, he is callously willing to let rivals kill each other off, so that he can solidify his holdings. The villain, however, wishes not only to do the same but also to capture the heroine by blackmailing her irresolute brother. So the hero decides to take sides. Not recommended.

On the other hand, *Borden Chantry* is an absorbing western detective story. Here L'Amour combines his knowledge of western life and his unforgotten ability as a former writer of hard-boiled detective short stories. The titular hero is a wiped-out cattleman turned Colorado town marshal. The reader may be interested to learn, at the halfway point of the novel, that the murder Borden must solve is that of Joe Sackett, whom L'Amour mentioned back in 1960 in *The Daybreakers* (but fails to mention in his *Sackett Companion*). Borden assembles his evidence and tracks the killer. Reader anxiety mounts when Tyrel Sackett gallops in, urges Borden to get cracking, and threatens to take over if he doesn't. Borden is endearing because of his modesty, and his situation is poignant because his wife, Bess (named Helen in *North to the Rails*), though loyal enough, cannot stand the snow and dust of the west and wants to go back to Vermont with their son, Tom (hero of the earlier-published *North to the Rails*). Nor does Bess cotton to the idea of her husband's interviewing local prostitutes to obtain vital evidence. Question: Why does anyone with magnificent Chantry blood coursing in his veins wish to remain in this locale? When Borden follows the killer into a landscape full of beautiful scenery, the answer is clear.

L'Amour worked hard on *Fair Blows the Wind*. It is one of his biggest novels to its date. The fact that it has 70 named characters, plus glimpses of a dozen or more historical personages, makes it a L'Amour blockbuster with almost the explosive power of the later *Bendigo Shafter, The Lonesome Gods, The Walking Drum,* and *Last of the Breed*. The geographic spread of *Fair Blows the Wind* is also impressive.

Fair Blows the Wind follows its hero from the west coast of England into northern Scotland, then to London and the Channel region, to the Azores and Spain and the Lowlands, then back to London, and on to the Carolinas and finally to Ireland. L'Amour is elusive about dates, giving several but not permitting the reader to pin down the action to a timetable. The main events occur about 1573–90. The narrative maintains a breathless pace but is weakened by one persistent fault— the careless handling of flashbacks. The first 6 chapters reveal Tatton Chantry marooned on a Carolina beach; then a 2-chapter flashback presents part of his childhood. So far, exciting. But then the resumed present too soon gives way to a 19-chapter flashback during which the stories are more exciting than Tatton's present, even when he falls in love on the beach. However, *Fair Blows the Wind* is a swashbuckling romp of great verve and suspense. It also has a hundred hints that are all bits of the Chantry jigsaw puzzle which would have been completed but for L'Amour's untimely death.[7]

The last novel of the Kilkenny series to be published is *The Mountain Valley War*. Taken together, the three are disappointing. L'Amour must have agreed, since he shelved Kilkenny. *The Mountain Valley War* offers little that is new: Kilkenny rides into southwestern Idaho to rest up, homestead, and build for a future that probably could never be secure. Here again, he puts his shining weapons at the service of justice. He cares for gun-orphaned kids, organizes nesters, boxes a heavy in town to attract legislative attention to regional problems, etc.

Two Blockbusters, Two Duds, and Two Sacketts

Next in order are *Bendigo Shafter* (1979), *The Proving Trail* (1979), *The Iron Marshal* (1979), *The Warrior's Path* (1980), *Lonely on the Mountain* (1980), and *Comstock Lode* (1981). The first and last of these, both monumental, show L'Amour's chronic ache to break out of the western mold. *The Proving Trail* and *The Iron Marshal* offer nothing new. And *The Warrior's Path* and *Lonely on the Mountain* continue the saga of the Sacketts, the first being about Barnabas's sons, Kin Ring and Yance, and the second being about Tell and his endangered cousin Logan in Canada.

Bendigo Shafter should become a classic western novel. It is a major work and a first-rate piece of fiction—one of the half-dozen most important books in L'Amour's career.[8] Totaling 47 chapters, it is longer than any of L'Amour's other books except the later *Comstock Lode* and the subsequent hardcovers. Further, it is more shapely than any of them. French-Canadian Bendigo Shafter narrates the story of his own maturing to responsible trail boss, town marshal, writer, New York visitor, and hunter and peacemaker among Indians. He came from humble beginnings as a teenage homesteader (beginning about 1862) in Wyoming's South Pass region, with his unhappily married brother Cain and his family, with widowed Ruth Macken and her son, and with a number of other town-building pioneers. This community of hardy souls runs the moral gamut from benign to depraved. It also boasts a pleasing spectrum of ages, from tots to nubile girls to adults to one person trying for patriarchal status. Nor does L'Amour neglect Indians both good and bad, Holy Rollers, claim jumpers, and renegades. His dramatis personae number more than 80. Disasters are numerous, but the good men and women who surrender to the beauty and power of nature win out. There are awesome challenges—a blizzard, hostile Indians, persons in need of rescue, building problems, a cattle drive from Oregon, gold and the wingless vultures it attracts, rustlers and other toughs, democracy vs. a kind of Plymouth Colony leadership system, a mountain lion, train-stalling buffalo, and even some Manhattan roughnecks. In spite of all that, there is surprisingly little violence. One scene is climaxed when Ben's strong brother stops a would-be gunman by seizing his hand and simply breaking it. Ben prevents injury to himself when in the East—by slugging one hired thug, getting the drop on his two associates, and ordering them at gunpoint to beat each other up conscientiously, all under the approving eye of an Irish policeman.

Bendigo Shafter has three balanced and numbered parts. The first part ends at the same time as Ben's youth does. In the second part, Ben goes to Oregon for cattle and enlists the aid of Uruwishi, "the Old One," an ancient Indian warrior emeritus and easily the finest person in the novel. In the third part, Ben resists the temptations of New York, returns to the pioneering town in the South Pass region but finds it half in decay, and heads with Uruwishi for the cleansing air of the sacred Indian Medicine Wheel in the Big Horn Mountains of Wyoming.

L'Amour flirts here again with including real-life characters, as he frequently does in his romantic historical reconstructions. He has Ethan Sackett say that he knew John Colter, legendary Yellowstone explorer who died in 1813. Another character, a recovering alcoholic gambler who takes up schoolteaching, says that he once met Edgar Allan Poe back in Philadelphia.[9] Ben converses with Horace Greeley in New York. Best of all, old Uruwishi remembers Lewis and Clark.

With *Bendigo Shafter* L'Amour may have signaled an intention to characterize women with greater care. His 19 named women in it range from Ruth Macken, perhaps suggested by early real-life Wyoming women politicians, to loyal homesteading wives, to the beautiful child-woman Ninon Vauvert. Ben is smitten by Ninon's charms, and she responds by precociously pledging her amorous loyalty to him. L'Amour often sends such girls out of the action, seemingly to avoid sexual encounters; in this case, Ninon goes to New Orleans and else-where to continue an acting career. Unusually open-ended, the novel trails off with more questions than answers about her future with Ben and about other matters as well. Thus it seems possible that L'Amour planned a sequel—but if so, he did not take the time to write it before he died.

The Proving Trail is a disquieting narrative of a teenage cowboy whose vacillating father's murder shoves the lad into many adventures, including abortive revenge, escape from relatives seeking his inheritance, contact with a pair of waitresses of contrasting personalities, and a nightmare sequence of episodic pursuits, flights, and fights. The novel, exciting when read but ridiculous when remembered, has a dozen authorial slips: a girl's aunt becomes her mother, a villain's wrist is broken but then evidently isn't, the hero presciently analyzes a seem-ing villain without evidence, an older brother drops four years in age, suppositions become facts with unerring certitude, a map stitched into a jacket materializes in a buckskin container, the hero vows not to talk then talks too much, he also vows not to shoot first then does so from ambush, and three pursuers inexplicably become four. More puzzling than all of this, however, is the hero's decision not to hate his father's killer after all, since everything is sort of inevitable. The best if strangest touch is L'Amour's inclusion of Haitian voodooism.

With *The Iron Marshal* L'Amour recovers his powers somewhat. Another western detective story, it has an impossibly complicated plot and is unique among L'Amour's works for opening in squalid lower Manhattan. Fleeing from a harsh charge of excusable homicide, young Tom Shanaghy finds himself on a westbound railroad train, from which he alights to danger. He saves a man from being lynched, then by improbable subterfuge and with impossible rapidity becomes the marshal of a lawless town in Kansas. Next, he pieces together evidence, including not only certain items pointing suspiciously at a woman but also jottings in a dead man's notebook, to solve L'Amour's most complex puzzle yet—nothing less than a triple cross.

Comstock Lode is an ambitious blockbuster. In it, the author sought to inject into the hero a degree of maturity often absent in early works. The novel features Val Trevallion, born in Cornwall, the son of migrating parents who are murdered en route to the Far West with Val, in search of a life better than what the tin mines back home could provide. Portuguese gold coins found submerged in the ocean off Cornwall have financed the little family's venture. That same gold lured a depraved killer and his gang to attack the Trevallions in Missouri. Later it will be yet more gold—the gold, and also the silver, of the fabulous Comstock Lode, discovered in June 1859—that will beckon L'Amour's cast of dozens, good and bad, to western Nevada.

L'Amour skillfully hardens Val Trevallion. He mines briefly for tin in Redruth, Cornwall, in 1849, when he is about 13. Later he travels to New Orleans and Westport, and he becomes an on-his-own orphan in Nevada. Ten years pass—too blankly—and Val, still eaten by a desire for revenge that he has only partially sated, arrives at glorious manhood. Versatile from having held many catch-as-catch-can jobs, he is now seen leaving the Sierras for Virginia City and the Lode. As in *Bendigo Shafter*, there is a traveling actress in *Comstock Lode*. She is the oddly named Grita Redaway, orphaned during the killers' attack in Westport but soon disappearing from Val's life, though never from his memory. As with Bendigo Shafter's love Ninon, so now with Grita: she travels far away, becomes a captivating actress, and returns like a happy fate to her never-lost love.[10] Grita's career in San Francisco theaters inspires some of L'Amour's finest local-color effects. But the young lady must go on tour to the Comstock Lode region, if L'Amour is to reunite her with Val. Just as she is in the process of doing so, and just as Val begins to fight the poisonous desire to continue with acts of vengeance, Grita happens to attract the eye of the villain. So it becomes Val's fate to be unable to avoid the consequences in his own psyche of the evil that the murderous gang inflicted—and its leader and remnants are fated themselves, that is, fated to attack Val before he can attack them.

L'Amour strives effectively for variety here—in locales, kinds of labor, types of women, and degrees of unsavoriness among the killers. One of the novel's major weaknesses, however, is the intrusion of incredible coincidence. Val unreasonably returns to the place where his father was killed, in Nevada; Grita follows New Orleans and Parisian successes with California performances and then comes to work near the Lode; minor characters knowing one main character each are pushed by chance into the path of other main characters; in the entire west, the killers the hero is seeking all filter back to Virginia City. Why don't the villains change their names and avoid their nemesis? L'Amour would have replied to this rational question by saying that these improbabilities are permissible because *Comstock Lode* is meant to be a latter-day Greek tragedy. Perhaps it is.

Bright Hero, Fine Heroine

Milo Talon (1981) and *The Cherokee Trail* (1982) came next. They are totally different novels.

At first glance, *Milo Talon* seems like an absorbing western detective novel—but not for anyone who has already read *The Man Called Noon, The Man from Skibbereen, Borden Chantry,* and *The Iron Marshal.* In large part, L'Amour reshaped old plot effects to create *Milo Talon.* Here is its plot in one unwieldy sentence, with numbers in place of characters' names, so as not to give it all away. Milo is hired by an evil man (#1) to find his "granddaughter" (#2), whose alleged inheritance he covets but who is really #3, the daughter of a strange man (#4, not #1's son, who is #5) and a woman (#6) who later married #7, a decent business rival of #1, but left him to wed #1's no-good son, whose father it becomes hero Milo's aim to thwart through kindled love for #8, whose mother (#9) kept house for deserted #7 so nicely that he willed her daughter a fortune, which is the object of ill-advised #1's greed but which "granddaughter" never inherited at all.

Although in most ways *Milo Talon* is a rather foolish work, it does generate and sustain an exciting sense of mystery, and there is chilling poetic justice in the way the villainess collides with a female sadist (#?) toward the macabre end.

The Cherokee Trail is different and more pleasing. The heroine Mary Breyton connives to grab the job of running a western stagecoach station in Colorado when her Union army officer husband is invalided out in the middle of the Civil War and then is killed heading west to take that job. Resourceful though she is, she must occasionally summon a good man to help out. Still, the way her ex-soldier father brought up his tomboyish daughter at Harlequin Oaks, their estate in Virginia, prepares her to be a self-reliant woman, western-style. At its healthy core, *The Cherokee Trail* is new and fresh. It is an au courant dramatization of successful minorities in western action: Mrs. Breyton is a widow now in the west and determined not to run back to Eastern security. She has a little daughter, Peg, rather than a son. The two are abetted loyally by Matty Maginnis, an Irish girl who decides to disembark from the stagecoach with Mary at Cherokee Station instead of going farther. For balance, L'Amour throws in two snooty daughters of a rich rancher who lives nearby. Another minority character is little Wat Turner, whose outlaw father has been killed and who turns up at Mary's station. At first the child is reluctant to accept aid from a mere woman; but before long he is cooperatively doing chores for his keep, flirting with Peg, and listening to fireside readings of Sir Walter Scott. Even the Indians in the immediate vicinity are now minorities. They watch, threaten a little, admire Mary's bravery, gobble up her cookies, and pay for them with antelope meat.

Mary Breyton is one of L'Amour's most engaging and active heroines. She works hard, sets a good example, demands and deserves respect, takes up weapons and uses them when she must, remains optimistic, lectures articulately and sweetly, and speaks movingly of her recollections of the good old days in Virginia. Further, being attractive as well as competent, she acts as a magnet for an interesting assortment of men with various attitudes toward her—attentive, flattering, watchful, doubtful, and even downright vicious.[11]

Pseudonymous Sacketts

The Shadow Riders (1982) seems for all the world like yet another Sackett segment, with the names of the main characters changed. Note that the reader is offered a Southern Ma and Pa, their three tough sons, a couple of pretty girls, and well-armed foes. Mac Traven could easily be Tell Sackett, while his brothers Dal and Jesse Traven are clones of Orrin and Tyrel Sackett. The resemblance is compounded for unrecovering L'Amour addicts by the fact that the TV version of *The Shadow Riders* starred Tom Selleck, Sam Elliott, and Jeff Osterhage as the Traven brothers, just as the TV miniseries called *The Sacketts* starred the same hirsute trio as the Sackett brothers. [12]

Once again, L'Amour avoids taking his hero through the Civil War, just as he reveals too little about Tell Sackett in the Civil War. Instead, the author has Union army Major Mac Traven returning home to Texas at war's end precisely in time to rescue his Confederate army brother Dal from renegade would-be lynchers. The novel then introduces the ugly subject of white slavery. Once home again, Mac and Dal learn that their brother Jesse has been wounded and abducted by ne'er-do-wells who have also grabbed their sister Gretchen, Dal's fiancée Kate, and several other attractive women for sale near Victoria, Texas. All of this lucrative crime takes place to support a mad Southern colonel's desire to continue fighting for what everyone else recognizes as a lost cause—the now-ended Civil War. What follows is exciting and vigorous, but almost never new for L'Amour readers. The cast of shopworn characters includes a lovable little girl and a semiretired pirate.

Chapter Six
L'Amour at Midnight

Three of the last eight novels by indefatigable L'Amour are as fine as anything he ever composed. They are *The Lonesome Gods* (1983), *The Walking Drum* (1984), and *Last of the Breed* (1986). Two other novels continue the Sackett saga. They are *Ride the River* (1983) and *Jubal Sackett* (1985), neither of which is very good. Two others are decidedly inferior pieces of work. They are *Son of a Wanted Man* (1984; original version, "The Trail to Peach Meadow Canyon," reprinted in *The Rider of the Ruby Hills*) and *Passin' Through* (1985). That leaves *The Haunted Mesa* (1987). Although it is a daring pioneer effort for the aging novelist to undertake, it shows too many signs of diminished creative control amid too few moments of excitement to be given a strong recommendation.

Yet, after all this, the indomitable L'Amour went ahead and put together *The Sackett Companion* (1988) and for good measure left *Education of a Wandering Man* on his desk at the time of his death.

Two Bull's-Eyes out of Four

The Lonesome Gods, which in a 1979 interview L'Amour said he had conceived 20 years earlier (Kalter, 4), became a money tree when it appeared as its author's first hardcover. His biggest book, it required careful research and composition. He moved slowly with it for a change. He studied the property-owning habits of the Cahuilla Indians, traveled Mojave and Colorado desert trails again, deepened his comprehension of ancient Indian markers there, and made the desert his story's true hero (*Gods,* 456–57). The divine spirit hovering over that heroic desert waits, sometimes in vain, to respond to those who revere it and worship in it. L'Amour's thesis is that "men need their gods, but did not the gods also need men?" (309). Here again is a young boy maturing painfully, becoming more aware, learning to love the best in life—physical prowess, the brooding land teeming with God's creatures, a good woman, male camaraderie, and wisdom in books. L'Amour praises solitude and silence, the sea, Oriental sensitiv-

ity, and patience. Who should not become patient in the face of
L'Amour's conclusion that often "man . . . may seem a fragment, a
chance object, a bit of flotsam on the waves of time" (342)?
The Lonesome Gods is a splendid novel. Its 61 chapters divide into
eight unnumbered parts. First (chapters 1–11), the hero Johannes
Verne, born in 1836, and his death-marked father escape into an empty
sanctuary. Second (chapters 12–17), Johannes survives a murderous attack and gets through the desert to Los Angeles. Third (chapters 18–
26), a magnificent woman, Miss Nesselrode, provides protection and
education for the boy, especially from his vicious Hispanic maternal grandfather, Don Isidro. Fourth (chapters 27–35), now mature,
Johannes gathers wild horses in the desert. Fifth (chapters 36–41), he
learns to fight and also falls in love. Sixth (chapters 42–47), he and his
friends pursue villains who have stolen his horse herd. Seventh (chapters 48–59), he is alone in the almost pitiless desert, but has friends,
and wins out at last. Eighth (chapters 60–61), coda. There are more
than 100 characters in *The Lonesome Gods*. As usual, L'Amour has problems with his jumping narrative point of view. He seems almost to
make a virtue of his inability to create a single filter or reflector for his
action and philosophizing. Johannes tells his story in all or parts of 52
chapters. But other narrators are occasionally enlisted to shed their
light, especially Miss Nesselrode,[1] Johannes's unreliable girlfriend,
Meghan Laurel, and evil Don Isidro, whom L'Amour sketches in grand
bold strokes.

L'Amour reaches for bizarre character combinations in *The Lonesome
Gods,* which includes a proud Spaniard who disowns his daughter,
seeks to kill his son-in-law and his grandson, abandons a son because
of his pathetic gigantism, and finds himself outmaneuvered by a weird
unmarried sister. Miss Nesselrode brings to California a bewildering
background, a hypnotic ability to control others—especially inimical
men and others whom she enlists to aid her Johannes—and also commercial savvy, which L'Amour painstakingly explains was more common in western women than standard history books admit. Long after
ordinary character and plot details of *The Lonesome Gods* fade from the
reader's mind, several things remain. The gods themselves, surely.
They are sad but immemorially patient, in the desert heat waves and
the cold mountain caves. A ghostly old Indian who has a triangular
blue stone suspended around his neck and who magically turns up to
aid Johannes from time to time. A wild black stallion that seems to
want his friendship. But most of all the family-abandoned giant—

tender, wise, stoical Alfredo. In time he knows that death is near for him and therefore seeks out an enormous stone seat high in the mountains where he can quietly watch the free eagles soar above him. This scene is one of the finest that L'Amour ever wrote. A rare rhetorical flourish in *The Lonesome Gods* is the hero's refrain, "I am Johannes Verne, and I am not afraid," which the lad repeats both when he is scared and after he proves his courage.[2] The refrain helps L'Amour create a fairy-tale atmosphere in *The Lonesome Gods*, which after all contains an evil grandfather, a ghost, a friendly horse, mysterious footprints, and a giant.

In sharp contrast to *The Lonesome Gods, Son of a Wanted Man* is a weak piece of fiction and in addition is badly edited. It has vague pronoun antecedents, absence of parallelism, mistakes such as "who" for "which" and "There's two," and gauche imagery, such as "a strange young bull . . . who had not won his spurs."[3]

The donnée of *Son of a Wanted Man* is clever and exciting. What kind of loyalty does an innocent young fellow owe to an outlaw who raised him thoughtfully? The novel opens with a practicing—though over-the-hill—western criminal calling for his technically spotless foster son to join him in a robbery. So far, a good western yarn; but after that the plot gets sloppy. Mike Bastin, age 22, has been trained only by lectures, map work, and dry runs along the outlaw to track, fight, and shoot. Suddenly, though never tested in dust, rain, and blood, he is asked to take over the leadership of a gang of real toughs, who the reader is invited to believe have been waiting for Mike to come and order them back into the bank- and train-robbing profession. Furthermore, the heroine has been kept in cellophane until the moment comes for her to meet the hero, who falls in love with her in about 10 minutes. These are two instances of unacceptable suspended narrative animation. Refreshing, though, is the reappearance of Borden Chantry and Tyrel Sackett, together again after their cooperative detective work in *Borden Chantry*. In a curiously staged penultimate climax,[4] the pair helps Mike foil an elaborate robbery attempt, after which Borden, in law-and-order L'Amour's harshest paragraph, answers a young criminal who is arrested after the shootout and asks what is in store for him: "Men who tried to steal the money others worked hard to earn got no sympathy from him [Borden]. 'For you? If you're lucky you may get no more than twenty years'" (*Son*, 150).

The Walking Drum, though not a western, may well be the best novel L'Amour ever wrote. It is a seafaring, overland-caravan, swashbuckling

romp starring the impossibly versatile Mathurin Kerbouchard. The son
of a missing Brittany corsair and a murdered mother, he is bent on
revenge, rescue, and adventure. He is also a sailor, horseman, swords-
man, archer, merchant, acrobat and juggler, magician and alchemist,
storyteller, lover (manqué, one should add), beggar, linguist (Arabic,
Frankish, Greek, Hindi, Latin, Persian, Sanskrit), botanist, pharma-
cist, gourmet, physician, surgeon, and demolition expert. He is also a
scholar who can memorize and then "copy" books on chemistry, geography, history, literature, military art, music, philosophy, and
religion.

The time of *The Walking Drum* is 1176–80. The place? Make that
places. The action starts on the coast of Brittany, proceeds to Spain
(Málaga, Cádiz, Córdoba, and Zaragoza), back to France and Flanders,
then by merchant caravan east to Kiev, thence down to the Black Sea
and Constantinople, Trebizond (Trabzon), and southeast to Tabriz,
Qazvin (Kazvin), and places better located on a map of *The Arabian
Nights*—though near enough in soiled spirit to modern-day Tehran,
Baghdad, and Basra. The main action occurs in Moorish Spain, Christian Paris and its environs,[5] the brutal Russia of the Petchenegs (fore-
runners of Mongol tribesmen), Byzantine Constantinople, and the
storied Seljuk Empire. Especially well evoked are Córdoba, Constantinople, and the Tabriz region.[6]

The Walking Drum, which gets its title from the cart-mounted drum
pounded to set the caravan's pace, divides into an introductory chapter
and then three fairly equal parts. The first part (chapters 2–23) concerns Kerbouchard's derring-do, amours (L'Amour is always timid on
this subject), scholarship (L'Amour is not timid enough here), and an-
tics in Spain. In the second part (chapters 24–42) the hero joins an
enormous merchant caravan weaving its way from fair to fair in western
Europe, then to Kiev, and encounters disaster on the shores of the
Black Sea. Always Kerbouchard seeks his father; so the third part
(chapters 43–57) takes him to Constantinople, to Tabriz and lovely
Princess Sundari Devi (from Anhilwara and heading back there in faraway Hind), and to the mountain fortress of Alamut in the Persian
Valley of Assassins. Does he find his father? I'll leave you to read the
novel to find out.

In the cast of characters are almost 80 people directly involved in
Kerbouchard's bellicose, scholarly, amorous, and picaresque activities.
Several of these personages are figures from history. They include Wil-
liam [II] of Sicily (?–1189); John of Seville (Johannes Hispalensus [fl.

mid-12th century]—Kerbouchard saves his life between Cádiz and Córdoba); Averroës ([1126–98]—Kerbouchard meets him at a party in Córdoba); Ibn-Beytar (Ibn-al-Baytar [?–1248]—could Kerbouchard have heard him discuss botany in Córdoba 70 years before his death?); Abul Kasim Khalaf (Abū-al-Qāsim [936?–1013?]—perhaps Kerbouchard met his grandson); Ibn-Quzman ([?–1060]—Kerbouchard could not have met this Arabian versifier and troubadour); Andronicus Comnenus ([1110–85], licentious cousin of Emperor Manuel I of Constantinople—Kerbouchard in 1180 correctly predicts to Andronicus that he will become emperor and be murdered by a mob—true, in 1183 and 1185); Emperor Emanuel I [Comnenus] of Constantinople ([1120?–80]—Manuel in real life was both more passive and sicker in 1180 than Kerbouchard notes); and Sinan ([?–1193], assassin leader from Basra during the time of Muhammad II [1166–1210]—L'Amour gives Sinan's full name as Rashid-Ad-din Sinan). Sinan is L'Amour's most fascinating real-life nonwestern character. He is a scholarly, hospitable leader of cruel assassins.[7]

Almost as important as the real-life Arabs whom Kerbouchard meets are the books he reads. A complete list of named sources of his wit, wisdom, history and scientific and literary lore, esoterica, and trivia would be not only too lengthy but also unbelievable. It is not to be countenanced that either Kerbouchard or L'Amour ever read with any degree of care one-twentieth of the items named in *The Walking Drum*. In the space of five chapters alone (chapters 43–47), L'Amour mentions works of Aristophanes, Firdausi, Virgil, Homer, Pytheus, Scylax, Eudoxus, Michael Psellus, Anna Comnena, Strabo, the Prince of Gurgan, Sun Tzu, Procopius, Menander, and Xenophon. Earlier, even more authors and titles are offered, including long-time L'Amour favorites al-Biruni, Plutarch, and Vegetius, and newcomers such as *The Ring and the Dove* and the rare *Ayennamagh*. (One set of books that L'Amour consulted has to do with costumes. A vivid and presumably accurate feature of *The Walking Drum* is its descriptions of clothing, materials, and accompanying armament.[8])

Kerbouchard is unique among L'Amour heroes. He is a rambling lover in search not of a new home but of an old father. So he loves the following ravishing beauties with never a thought of settling down: Aziza of Palermo, met at sea off Málaga; Sharaza, a brigand's daughter in the mountains outside Córdoba; Valaba, a mysterious Córdoba hostess; Safia, a Córdoba spy from Shiraz; Comtesse Suzanne de Malcrais, met near Provins, outside Paris, but wanted for a political marriage back in Saône, near Antioch; and the incomparable Sundari Devi, met at Tabriz but wanted for an arranged marriage back in Anhilwara. There may be too much truth for comfort in Suzanne's jibe at Kerbouchard: "You have spoken so much of that [lovemaking] . . . that I wonder if you are not just a talker."[9] *The Walking Drum* contains more talk about lips, bosoms, thighs, hips, intimacy, and sex than all the rest of L'Amour's books combined. In addition, the word "fornicates" appears here (454), and the threat of castration figures in the plot.

L'Amour once happily confessed that "[w]riting *The Walking Drum* was pure pleasure" (*Education,* 190). It is spiced with wild adventures told at a galloping pace, a dozen grand climaxes, and splashy landscapes rolling after one another fast enough to remind one of Cinerama. It is perhaps ungracious to add that the novel is weakened by improbable coincidences, undigested background reading, generalizations (often charmingly archaic in diction but eventually tedious in content), and wretched copyediting.

Kerbouchard is a survivor cast in the mold of epics of yore. So the reader expects him to be slashed in the face, skull, and thigh, to be struck across the bridge of his nose, arrowed in the side, and cast on a fire for dead, to have a horse step on his foot, and to lose at least a fingernail during a climb up a cliff. Moreover, he is a captivating combination of cinematic star, dream lover, and scholarly name-dropper. Therefore, it was tragic that death prevented L'Amour from completing his promised Middle Eastern medieval trilogy, in which his hero would have loved and been wounded some more.

Late in life, L'Amour surrendered again to the temptation to palm off a second-rate short novel after a splendid longer effort. He had done so by following *The Lonesome Gods* with *Son of a Wanted Man.* Then, sure enough, in the wake of *The Walking Drum* came *Passin' Through.*

Passin' Through is a pleasant mystery yarn, but with old familiar tangles. The engagingly slow-witted, folksy narrator is called "Passin' Through" because—if you have not guessed already—he wants nothing so much as to keep on passin' through. Specifically, he would like to ride northeast of the Four Corners of Utah, Colorado, New Mexico, and Arizona, into high altitudes, solitude, and peace of mind. But on the way he stops at Parrott City for a little drink. A saloon bully's conversation is so impolite that the narrator has to stop it with a fatal throat shot. He is promptly hanged, abandoned while still kicking, and rescued by two Indians; he then escapes on what must be defined as a magic horse to a ranch claimed by a secretly vicious woman named

Mrs. Dory Hollyrood. Matty Higgins, her scared young servant girl (whose father knew Parmalee Sackett, as the reader is informed for no reason), also lives there. Both females are attractive to the hero. So "Mr. Passin'," as Dory calls him once he agrees to linger and tidy her spread for a while, temporarily restrains his restless urge to move on, keeps his own counsel, solves a mystery that most readers could figure out 10 chapters before he does, and then . . . ?

Loyal L'Amour fans will recognize many old landmarks in *Passin' Through*: hero as boy killed father's killer; hero hankers to settle down; hero stops to help women (both former actresses); hero finds evidence-crammed cattleman's tally book; etc. Such fans will also recognize familiar stylistic watermarks: repeated use of the words *eye, home, lonely, silence,* and *trouble*; Anglo-Saxon rhythms ("Cold was the moon rising . . . and cold the wind that whispered," "Slow passed the moonlit night, slow came the dawn," and "Long stretched the night, and cold and wet I longed for the dawn,"[10] etc.); compositional and grammatical errors, allied infelicities echoed from earlier works, and mind-numbing clichés; and plot-sedating lectures on western trivia and explanations of how real-life people such as Chris Madsen, Langford Peel, Bill Tilghman, Luke Short, Billy the Kid, and Pat Garrett were behaving at about the time of the story (summer 1881). It seems certain that *Passin' Through,* like several other so-so L'Amour titles from the mid-1980s, was a dusted-off and insufficiently polished chestnut from L'Amour's apprentice years.

Final Encores

With *Last of the Breed* and *The Haunted Mesa* L'Amour ventured into new realms. The first succeeds with great gusto, while the second has only moments of triumph.

In *Last of the Breed,* L'Amour gives us an eastern Siberian western. Fort Yuma becomes Colonel Arkady Arkadovich Zamatev's Soviet-intelligence prison camp east of Lake Baikal. The endangered hero is Major Joseph "Joe Mack" Makatozi, a Sioux-Cheyenne U.S. Air Force pilot snatched by the dread GRU (worse even than the KGB), Soviet mind-benders bent on picking his brain for Yankee technology. The time is not long before the novel's 1986 publication date, since mention is made of the ongoing Soviet-Afghanistan War (from 27 December 1979), the shooting down by the Soviets of the South Korean jetliner (30 August 1983), and [Mikhail S.] Gorbachev (in power starting 11 March 1985). Joe Mack's escape route is not over or through anything so mild as the Rockies or Death Valley; instead, he traverses about 2,000 miles (usually on foot but also by stolen car and borrowed helicopter) of the Yablonovy, Stanovoy, Verkhoyansk, Chersky, Kolyma, and Koryak mountains, ever eastward toward the Bering Strait. Readers having trouble keeping track of the more than 80 place names dotting this novel may consult its endpaper maps—not of Apache Territory or Durango this time, but of haunting Siberia.

And hauntingly beautiful, as well as unforgiving, it is. The two heroes of *Last of the Breed* are long-lasting Joe Mack and everlasting Siberia. Joe adapts atavistically to its terrain, animals, trees, water, and spirit.[11] He responds to a woman, too. She is not a Big Sky schoolmarm, a Long Branch hostess, or an Arizona widow lady, but Natalya "Talya" Baronas, member of a fur-trapping band driven into exile by the long-term political and cultural consequences of Karl Marx and Joseph Stalin. They are willing not only to feed but also to be fed by the resourceful trapper Mack. And who tracks him? Alekhin, a hooded-eyed Yakut so formidable that he can follow his quarry over icy rocks in the twilit taiga near the Arctic Circle. Although Alekhin is as big as a grizzly, Joe Mack, even after four seasons on the run and thinned down from his predictable 6 feet, 2 inches and 190 pounds, is not at all reluctant to turn from hunted to hunter in classic formulaic western fashion.

Throughout *Last of the Breed,* L'Amour persuades the reader to suspend his disbelief and accept as credible a simplistic, *Rambo*-type plot. He is successful in doing so partly because his outdoor Siberia is totally credible, as are most of his preglasnost, preperestroika Soviets. They experience the same emotions, good and bad, that his traditional western characters do. Unfortunately, he could not break himself of the habit of lecturing his audience, even though his podium was not placed in nineteenth-century America or the twelfth-century Middle East but in the twentieth-century Soviet Union. This time around, his topics are Russian flora and fauna, Russian history, the Cold War, and—fascinatingly, given the crumbling of communism in the Soviet Union and Eastern Europe in the 1990s—his solution (in 1986) to the thawing Cold War: tear down the Berlin Wall, exchange technological information, and open up Siberia, especially Lake Baikal and the Kamchatka Peninsula, to moneyed American tourists.[12]

Last of the Breed should be criticized for having too many pages and too little variety. In 28 of its 47 chapters, Joe Mack is alone, on half-

frozen feet in homemade moccasins most of the time, and in temper-
atures down to $-50°$ to $-80°$ F. L'Amour also handles point-of-view
shifts choppily. Two examples: "It was the Tsipa [River], but this he
[Joe Mack] did not know"; and "What he did not know was that Alekhin had landed."[13] Since the hero is central, it is hard for the reader to
follow plot lines concerning 40 other characters, including villains and
their adversaries, exiles and dissidents, Zamatev's mistress, government workers and army officers, a jealous trapper, a frightened fur
dealer, and Talya's professor father (smart because not American). In
sum, *Last of the Breed* is a big novel, with a big hero and a big cast,
cast in a big land.

L'Amour prepared his readers for *The Haunted Mesa* in some measure
by writing *The Californios* and *The Lonesome Gods,* which also touch on
supernaturalism. But when L'Amour published the last two books, he
was in better control of his powers. He also previewed the central subject of *The Haunted Mesa* when he included "The Old Ones" in *Frontier,*
his 1984 book of essays. The Old Ones are better known as the Cliff
Dwellers, of the Four Corners area of the Southwest, and are more
technically called the Anasazi. *The Haunted Mesa* as a novel is compar-
atively unsuccessful; yet one must accord the aging writer genuine
praise, for he innovatively grounds it both in science fiction and in
Indian and Latin-American mythology (see *Companion,* 81). Its hero
Mike Raglan is a partly autobiographical figure. He was orphaned at
12, worked on a ranch and in a circus, mined along the Colorado River,
traveled to Sinkiang, Tibet, and elsewhere, learned Arabic, and began
extensive research into the occult. In the course of the next 20 years,
he made himself into an investigator of extrasensory phenomena. Then,
one day, he answered an appeal from his friend Erik Hokart to come
from New York to southeastern Utah and help him check into something strange. Thus L'Amour's last novel published in his lifetime
begins.

What Mike steps into is not only the space but also occasionally the
time of the Anasazi, cliff-dwelling pre-Navajos who once lived west of
what archaeologists now call the Cedar Mesa Province and north of the
Navajo Mountain Province. Their homeland once covered an elliptical
area in what is now southern Utah, southwestern Colorado, and into
Arizona and New Mexico, with many modern cities—such as Flagstaff,
Arizona; Gallup, Albuquerque, and Santa Fe, New Mexico; and Durango, Colorado—now within their former borders. (In the novel, mention is made of Durango, Navajo Mountain [on the Utah-Arizona

border], Monticello [Utah], and Medicine Hat [Utah].) According to
L'Amour's endpaper maps, his fictitious "Haunted Mesa" is the west-
ern point of an equilateral triangle, the other points of which are Mesa
Verde (Colorado) and De Chelly (Arizona).

The Anasazi vanished in the thirteenth century without a trace. Theories differ as to why their immemorially old civilization ended. An-
thropologist Fred Plog suggests "death, migration, or aggregation into
larger sites" as possible causes, but he admits that not even "death,
disease, invasion, warfare, and climatic change" can fully explain the
mystery.[14] Novelist and scholar Tony Hillerman, in a review of *The
Haunted Mesa*, suggests mythopoetic possibilities: perhaps God ordered
the Anasazis to migrate; maybe they were enslaved by a supernatural
entity; possibly a whirlwind destroyed them; a prolonged drought
could have starved them; or did fierce nomads invade and wipe them
out? He adds that "L'Amour, whose Colorado ranch [near Durango]
has Anasazi ruins on three sides of it, has a better idea," and specifies
what it is: "In *The Haunted Mesa*, L'Amour solved the mystery of what
happened to the Anasazis by postulating *sipapus* ['a sort of birthing
passage from the womb of earth'] which operates both ways—making
them gates between this Fourth World of ours and the evil Third
World [in Anasazi history]."[15]

The donnée here is intriguing, but the novel based on it is somewhat
disappointing. True, his Mike jumps through a kiva time-window into
"the Other Side," and finds it populated not only by good Anasazi
Indians but also by evil Indians with Mayan connections. Sure enough,
the good Indians have survived after disappearing, all this time. But
are L'Amour's heroine Kawasi and her people evil "time warpers," from
seven centuries back? In any event, Mike storms the Aztec- and Mayan-
type City of the Forbidden to rescue Erik, kidnapped from his mesa
digs by Kawasi's foes in need of his electronics expertise to update their
telepathic powers.[16]

This summary may suggest that *The Haunted Mesa*, which has 43
short chapters, is exciting. It is not, at least, not until its real beginning, which may be in chapter 9 or 13—or perhaps 20, to be truthful.
Mike obtains Erik's diary but then foolishly reads it only sporadically,
rehashes his options and evidence too often (chapter 25 could be en-
tirely deleted), shuttles tediously from motel to mesa (until chapter
29), and presents innumerable lectures—about scientific oddities, faraway places, the advantages of being a World War II veteran, the in-
evitability of intellectual evolution, "parallel worlds," dogs, and so

on.[17] There are other flaws. The novel has only four important white characters (two of whom are introduced late), only four important Indians from "the Other Side" of time (two of whom appear late), too little dialogue (and some breaking into action and awkwardly suspending it), and a love affair both tardy and perfunctory. One unforgettable scene, however, makes up for many weaknesses. During a "timequake"—rather than an earthquake—one villain gets stuck between times and looks somewhat the way Oscar Wilde's youthful Dorian Gray would if smashed over the head with his own aging portrait. What a challenge for the moviemakers!

Last Book and a Half

Shortly before his death, L'Amour completed *The Sackett Companion: A Personal Guide to the Sackett Novels* (published November 1988) and drafted *Education of a Wandering Man* (published November 1989).

The Sackett Companion is the most personally revealing of L'Amour's books. It contains autobiographical anecdotes and asides about his experiences while he was working and wandering in the Far West during his youth and about western old-timers he bumped into and pumped for information. L'Amour also includes historical data gleaned from western documents both standard and arcane, tour-guide trivia, and comments on the fun and problems he encountered and techniques he developed while composing one Sackett volume after another. L'Amour coquettishly mixes remarks about the doings of his Sackett characters with veracious historical items, as though his Sacketts were as true as Pikes Peak.

The Sackett Companion is typical of L'Amour. To begin with, its logic is more apparent than real. It treats one Sackett title after another, in chronological order not of publication but of events in the narrative sequence. Individual sections of the book, however, are not logical. Encyclopedia-like entries (some woefully skimpy) of persons, places, and things are neither alphabetically nor chronologically arranged, nor even in the order those items appear in the novels under consideration. This book also contains innumerable composition errors that an experienced western writer should have learned to avoid decades earlier. Moreover, the index would have been more useful if it had not been incomplete. Partly making up for these problems, however, are a Sackett family tree and a series of maps, essential for anyone interested in pinning down areas of Sackett action. Portions of the text and the

family tree also hint (sadly, in retrospect) that L'Amour had several
more Sackett volumes in mind.

Education of a Wandering Man was left in the rough at the time of
L'Amour's death. If the author had been able to revise the book with
honest care, the results would have added to our knowledge of his life
and of the smorgasbord of western and Far Eastern writings that mattered to him as a novelist. As it is, however, the book is an embarrassment. It is not much more than a rambling journal, badly edited and
sadly unindexed. It should not have been released by L'Amour's heirs
for publication.[18]

In it, L'Amour had four purposes: to identify the educative jobs that
he held during his "knockabout" years and later, until his marriage; to
name numerous books (but providing no in-depth discussion) that he
had read during his youth and early maturity; to reveal (with a modesty
more apparent than genuine) his self-reliance, vocational versatility,
physical prowess, memory, and writing ability; and, worst of all, to
offer capsule theories on dozens of subjects. The result is neither detailed autobiography nor a useful reading list.

The 28 disjointed chapters of *Education of a Wandering Man* fail to
coalesce into any semblance of unity. L'Amour introduces a given subject early and drops it for a while, repeats himself, is furtive with dates
and data, embarrasses the knowledgeable, and teases the ignorant. He
might have captivatingly combined autobiographical material in
chronological order, analysis of his own fiction, and real discussions of
his most enjoyable reading. (He is to be doubted when he claims to
have carefully read 100 books a year and skimmed innumerable others—when hoboing on boxcars, after work in lumber camps, driving
to Oklahoma with his parents, having just retreated from the Battle of
the Bulge area, etc.). Here are a few embarrassing little instances.
L'Amour mentions James Gillette twice, both times only in passing
(33, 183). Twice he says he wants to succeed only with old-timers who
will first read him, then finger the text, and finally say, "Yes, that is
the way it was," and "That was how it was" (142, 220). He writes,
"In that one year I reviewed twenty-two books" (138) but does not
specify the year. (It was 1937.) He mentions his "wife" and names a
"Kathy," but not in the same paragraph and not to join the two (32).
His comments on *Hamlet,* Edgar Allan Poe, Friedrich Wilhelm
Nietzsche, Joseph Conrad, Eugene O'Neill, Jack London, Hervey Al-
len, etc. range from the negligible to the gauche. He names a score of
Far Eastern works, authors, and authorities (including [Henri] Cordier

and [Sir Henry] Yule, Sir Alexander Cunningham, J. Evetts Haley, I-Tsing, *Malay Annals,* Nagarjuna, *Outlaws of the Marsh,* and Sir Aurel Stein), but his comments are random and sparse. He cites more than a dozen of his own titles but elucidates nothing. The following is typical. Complaining that he would prefer to be called a "frontier" rather than "a western writer," he elaborates on the distinction without really clarifying it: "Much of my writing has to do with men on the western frontier, even when that frontier was east of the Appalachians, as in *Sackett's Land, To The Far Blue Mountains,* and *The Warrior's Path.* (Two of these stories begin in Elizabethan England, incidentally, as does *Fair Blows the Wind*) (155). The book also includes tedious boasts such as "I have delved deeply into the literatures of the world" and "I have made no effort to gather the so-called great books [into his personal library]. Most of them I read during my knockabout years" (120, 199).[19]

Education of a Wandering Man is an unintentionally revealing book that might have been a document of great importance in the study of pop culture in America, if L'Amour had lived long enough to revise it into a more coherent and connected form.

Chapter Seven
The Family Sagas

L'Amour published 17 novels concerning members of the Sackett family sprawling over three centuries and two continents, 5 novels about his Chantry family, and 3 novels about his Talons. He promised many more, especially about his popular Sackett men. For example, he announced plans to cast Sacketts and Chantrys in an American Revolutionary War novel together and to detail Tell Sackett's Civil War career and his first love affair. L'Amour's Sackett people were supposed to intermarry with his Chantry people, probably late in the nineteenth century. Further, the author promised to explain about the progenitor of his Talons—Talon the Claw, a one-handed pirate, millionaire, and Gaspé settler in the sixteenth century. When L'Amour was writing *The Sackett Companion,* probably 1987 and early 1988, he was still hoping to fill out no less than 10 generations of Sacketts, many of whom he unfortunately did not live to bring to life. A glance at "The Sackett Family Tree" (*Companion,* [254–55]) will give the reader a notion of the audacity of L'Amour's plan. If completed—and combined with less ambitious but still heady ideas for his Chantrys and Talons—his three-family mega-saga might have totaled almost 50 books.

Literary Brethren

Many authors have been as ambitious as L'Amour in writing family series with reappearing characters, fiction that attempts to depict a historical epoch in a given region, and the like. Examples include James Fenimore Cooper, Honoré de Balzac, Emile Zola, Anthony Trollope, John Galsworthy, and William Faulkner.[1]

L'Amour's story of Tell Sackett and his brothers, like Cooper's Leatherstocking volumes, is told out of chronological order but traces the characters as they move ever westward. Balzac was also influenced by Cooper, and the contours of his *Comédie Humaine* may have influenced L'Amour. Balzac created more than 500 *personnages reparaissants,* whose reappearances in various novels help unify his vast body of writings.

He employed the device of "indeterminacy," which obliges readers to exercise their imagination in filling gaps between the stories. Balzac also shifts his narrative point of view, to help his readers see that ideas must be studied from several angles. These devices are what one critic has called "means for evoking a sustained, almost obsessive interest in the reader."[2] L'Amour has reappearing Sacketts, Chantrys, and Talons by the squads; and hints in publicity blurbs and *The Sackett Companion* created exciting indeterminacy for his readers, which his death frustrated.

Zola, whom L'Amour mentions in *Shalako* and *Kilrone,* set an example for L'Amour by making his Rougon-Macquart novels a connected series. Zola followed Balzac's lead in using reappearing characters and unified his 20 books in the series by having them illustrate the transmission of hereditary traits through 30 or so family members in five generations. Parallels to L'Amour are again noticeable. In addition, Zola had a relationship with his publisher as productive as that of L'Amour with his, if not so profitable: Zola promised a dozen novels (each longer than L'Amour's paperbacks) in six years. So each man was prolific. The unity of L'Amour's family sagas is not the result of any theory of heredity, but informing those novels are the notions that the settlement of the western frontier in America catalyzed saliently good and bad traits in the American character, that only the strongest survived, and that the western movement illustrates a kind of Manifest Destiny. Further, most of L'Amour's Sacketts, Chantrys, and Talons are tall, strong males—perhaps symbolic of the frontier's dominant forces in action. Three times in *Sackett's Land* L'Amour mentions the dynastic pioneering destiny of the Sackett clan. In due time, Tell Sackett reports, "We Sacketts were healthy breeders, running long on tall boys. Counting ourselves, we had forty-nine brothers and cousins. Starting a feud with us didn't make any kind of sense. If we couldn't outshoot them we could outbreed them" (*Sackett,* 21). Later he opines that he will "fight back" because "it was bred in the bloodline of those from whom I come, and I could not be other than I am."[3]

Trollope is the novelist whose writing regimen L'Amour's most closely paralleled. In 36 years Trollope produced 63 works in 129 volumes. In his *Autobiography* he explains that he was at work early each morning at 5:30, wrote 250 words per quarter-hour by the watch on his desk, and produced 10 pages a day for 10 months a year. That meant 3 fat novels a year normally. He could compose anywhere—at home, at his club, on a train, aboard ship. Such work habits greatly

resemble L'Amour's. Further, Trollope's Barsetshire Chronicles, in six
novels, are similar to L'Amour's Sackett works; and Trollope's Parlia-
mentary Series novels detail activities of 10 recurring characters, who
also appear in 6 other works, including a pair of Barsetshire books.[4]
All of this is analogous to L'Amour's habit of having Sacketts pop up
in non-Sackett novels.

Many authors have been inspired swiftly and surely, just as L'Amour
was. John Galsworthy once said that getting the idea on 28 July 1918
for *The Forsyte Saga* was the happiest day of his writing life. Both Balzac
and Zola had similar epiphanic moments during which they saw major
phases of their lifework in a flash.[5] Likewise, L'Amour could recall the
moment he had been inspired to start his Sackett-clan tales. In Tuc-
umcari, New Mexico, he was getting the better of a fellow in a scrap
when two of the loser's 29 cousins from two families began to pitch in
loyally. "So I began thinking about it [L'Amour reports] and I decided
to write a story about a family like that, where whenever one of them
was in trouble all the others always came to help."[6] L'Amour later
offered a different version of this anecdote, when he recalled that after
outboxing a rowdy in an unnamed town in New Mexico, he was saved
by two fellows who were cousins and who explained to L'Amour that
they never were lured into such fights because potential opponents
were aware that the pair came from two families with 29 young males
(*Companion*, 8–10).

Galsworthy also resembled L'Amour in the pacing of his output. *The
Forsyte Saga* coalesced from 1906 through 1921, after which Galsworthy continued the Forsyte story in 5 more works of fiction making up
A Modern Comedy (1929) and closed with some Forsyte short stories 3
years after that—25 years in all. L'Amour began his Sackett series with
The Daybreakers in 1960 and published the last Sackett segment he
lived to write, *Jubal Sackett,* in 1985, 25 years later.

Differences of substantive and stylistic elements apart, the works of
William Faulkner and L'Amour are alike in several respects. Faulkner
vitalized a section of America's Deep South and populated a few centuries of it with family forebears and members of the Compson,
McCaslin, Sartoris, Snopes, Stevens, and Sutpen clans, among other
families of other races. L'Amour vitalized our South, Far West, and
Northwest by depicting American Indians, whites, and Hispanics in
friendship and strife over a few centuries as well. Both authors praise
dignity, courage, endurance, the art of prevailing in the battle of good

against evil, and the joy of worshiping the precious soil of the New World.

Sackett Series Dramatis Personae

L'Amour's 17 Sackett novels, in order of publication, are *The Daybreakers* (1960), *Sackett* (1961), *Lando* (1962), *Mojave Crossing* (1964), *The Sackett Brand* (1965), *Mustang Man* (1966), *The Sky-Liners* (1967), *The Lonely Men* (1969), *Galloway* (1970), *Ride the Dark Trail* (1972), *Treasure Mountain* (1972), *Sackett's Land* (1974), *To the Far Blue Mountains* (1976), *The Warrior's Path* (1980), *Lonely on the Mountain* (1980), *Ride the River* (1983), and *Jubal Sackett* (1985).

If the same novels are arranged in the chronological order of their events, the relative positions are certain for 13—*Sackett's Land, To the Far Blue Mountains, Jubal Sackett, The Warrior's Path, Ride the River, The Daybreakers, Lando* (which starts after *The Daybreakers* but ends before *The Sackett Brand*), *Lonely on the Mountain, Sackett, Mojave Crossing, The Sackett Brand, The Lonely Men,* and *Treasure Mountain.* There are problems about the other 4: *Ride the Dark Trail* takes place after *The Sackett Brand; The Sky-Liners,* after *The Daybreakers* and *The Sackett Brand; Galloway,* after *The Sky-Liners*; and *Mustang Man,* shortly after *The Daybreakers.*

In these novels are more than 50 Sackett characters, including the active ones and also ancestors named, in-laws named or hinted at, and a few noisy young ones. In "The Sackett Family Tree" in L'Amour's *Sackett Companion* are 64 Sacketts, 4 of whom are given numbers, not names. Some of the numbers may refer to more than one child, thus perhaps increasing the clan population above 64. The tree started with Ivo and Megan Sackett in Elizabethan England. Their son Barnabas, who married Abigail Tempany, eventually had 4 sons, Kin Ring, Brian, Yance, and Jubal, and a daughter, Noelle. (Brian and Noelle return to England with their mother, and disappear not only from the later published novels but also evidently from L'Amour's plans for future novels.)

L'Amour developed many descendants of Kin Ring and Yance into superb fictional characters. But others, often named, he did not manage to put into novels before he died. Here is the record of what he both accomplished and planned. Kin Ring marries Diana Macklin, and their children are Malaby, Bretton, Ann, and Philip. A descendant of

Malaby and Vanora Sackett is Daubeny Sackett, four generations later. He marries Nata and becomes the father of Mawney, Regal, Pym, and John. Mawney (husband of Fiora Clyde Sackett) becomes the father of Echo, Ethan, and Colborn. Pym (husband of Cindy Larraway Sackett) becomes the father of Falcon and other children. John (husband of Willie Mae Calvin Sackett) becomes the father of Buckley. Next, the son of Mawney is Colborn, who marries Mary Ann and becomes the father of Orrin, Bob, Joe, Tyrel, and William Tell. Falcon marries Aleyne Kurbishaw, and their son is Orlando ("Lando"). Falcon later marries Virginia ("Gin") Locklear; they have no children. Buckley marries Nan Mackaskill, and their sons are Flagan and Galloway. Kin Ring's son Phillip marries Ruth Bernard, and their descendant seven generations later is Parmalee Sackett. Yance marries Temperance Penney, and their children are Boyne and others not named. A descendant of Boyne, three generations later, is Shandy Sackett, and he and his wife Huguette have a son named Tarbil, whose son Thomas is the father of twin sons, Logan and Nolan. Jubal marries Itchakomi Ishaia, whose child L'Amour never officially named. Yance and his progeny are Clinch Mountain Sacketts; Kin Ring and his progeny, Cumberland Hills Sacketts; and Philip and his progeny, Flatland Sacketts. The family tree displays full names of five Sacketts who are incompletely named in the 17 novels. They are Buckley, Colborn, Mary Ann, Megan, and Nata. New names are those of eight other Sacketts. They are Fiora Clyde, Nan Mackaskill, Mawney, Philip, Ruth Bernard, Thomas, Vanora, and Willie Mae Calvin.

This is still not the total. Alongside the family tree but not in it, L'Amour discusses seven other characters. They are Mordecai, Macon, and Trulove Sackett, Emily Sackett and her husband, Reed Talon, and their children, Barnabas, Milo, and four others not given first names. Of these four, L'Amour says, "Their exact connection to the rest of the Sacketts remains to be revealed" (*Companion,* 254). In addition, diligent readers of L'Amour's Sackett novels may recall the names Packet Sackett[7] and Seth Sackett.[8] In his *Sackett Companion,* L'Amour says nothing about Packet but reports that Seth was a real-life Colorado explorer unrelated to his fictional characters (256). It seems chauvinistic of L'Amour to keep three of the four named daughters of Sacketts childless; however, he may have done so to prevent the family tree from becoming too complicated by descendants with differing surnames. Whatever the reason, there are no family-tree branches of descent from Noelle, Anne, or Echo; Emily is the exception. (Feminists will dislike

Jubal Sackett's explanation to Itchakomi, an Indian woman, that in white society "rank descends through the man"; but feminists may also smile at her reply: "Hah! You must trust your women very much."[9])

Surrounding all of these Sacketts are close to 750 characters, including historical figures added for verisimilitude and to heighten action. If completed, the Sackett saga would of course have been even more impressively panoramic. L'Amour himself rashly asserted that "the story of the Sackett family has only begun" (*Companion,* 257).[10]

It is more important to consider fleshed-out fiction rather than skeletal plans. Most of L'Amour's readers are Sackett worshipers, not genealogists; so for information about the clan they rely on the 17 novels, not *The Sackett Companion.* Moreover, the novels are exciting, whereas the *Companion,* though fun, is also frustrating.

William Tell Sackett is L'Amour's most important Sackett. Tell narrates 6 of the novels: *Sackett, Mojave Crossing, The Lonely Men, Treasure Mountain, Lonely on the Mountain,* and *The Sackett Brand.* He often hints at the spread and loyalty of his clan. For example, he says, "I've never seen more than a dozen [Sacketts] at one time except when great-grandpa and great-grandma [Daubeny and Nata] had their wedding anniversary. There were more than a hundred men. I did not count them all" (*Treasure,* 26). And he warns would-be assailants: "If they get me, there's fifty, maybe a hundred more Sacketts. They'll hear of it, and they will come ridin'. . . . [W]hen somebody kills a Sackett he buys grief and death and disaster" (*Brand,* 99).

Not until *Sackett's Land,* the twelfth Sackett novel, did L'Amour present the patriarch of the clan, Barnabas Sackett. He is depicted in 1599 as coming from the Cambridgeshire fenlands and wanting to "found a family . . . but not with a sword." Nor does he wish to stay in the undemocratic Old World. Once he gets to the New World, he says, "This land was my destiny" and "This was the land!"[11] Oddly, after he and his marvelous wife, Abigail (daughter of an Elizabethan sea captain), fulfill a prophecy voiced in *To the Far Blue Mountains* and have sons Kin Ring (hyphenated as Kin-Ring beginning in *Jubal Sackett*), Brian, Yance, and Jublain (called Jubal), and daughter Noelle, Barnabas becomes passive in Carolina. He lets Abigail, Brian, and Noelle return to London, then acts out another prophecy by deliberately walking into an Indian ambush, sword in hand and with flames leaping about him.

But the dynasty spreads through Kin and Yance. Yance, wild and bushy-browed, roves to Massachusetts, gets into trouble, and is put in the stocks. Temperance likes, rescues, and elopes with him in *To the Far Blue Mountains.*[12] Kin pursues Temperance's Cape Ann friend Diana Macklin, a modern and scholarly girl who has been snatched for the Jamaican white-slave trade. After a slapdash rescue, the two are married in a beautiful Carolina-beach ceremony by a nautical minister whom Barnabas saved in Newfoundland and who married Kin's parents in *The Warrior's Path.*

It is owing to Yance and Temperance that the Tennessee Sacketts multiply. As Tell reminds the reader a couple of centuries later, "ol' Yance . . . founded the [Clinch Mountain] line way back in the 1600s."[13] But more details would have been helpful about the forebears of the Cumberland, Tennessee, Sacketts (Tell, Orrin, Tyrel, Bob, and Joe), of the Denney's Gap Sacketts (Flagan and Galloway), of Falcon and his son Orlando (from South Carolina, the Blue Ridge region, and Clinch's Creek), of Parmalee (from Arizona and New Mexico), of Emily (who through marriage helps connect some Sacketts to some Talons), and Echo (from Tuckalucky, Tennessee). The finished fiction does not address these problems. L'Amour in *Mojave Crossing* clarifies to a degree what still remains partly obscure when he has Tell say that "there were three kinds of Sacketts in Tennessee. The Smoky Mountain Sacketts, the Cumberland Gap Sacketts, and the Clinch Mountain Sacketts. These here last ones [Tell adds], they were a mean outfit and we had no truck with them unless at feuding time, where we were always pleased to have them on our side.[14] For geographic details, the reader is referred to maps in *The Sackett Companion* (62, 84, 117).

Hints in the fiction permit the conclusion that Tell's generation of Sackett fighting males are mostly "cousins." In *Treasure Mountain* the reader learns that Orlando is Tell's cousin. In *Mustang Man* Nolan mentions "a cousin of mine . . . named Tyrel."[15] In *Galloway,* Flagan explains that he and his brother, Galloway, are Tell's cousins; in the same novel, Parmalee corrects the rumor that he and Galloway are cousins by saying, "Second cousins, I believe."[16] For good measure, in *The Man from the Broken Hills* (not a Sackett novel), Milo Talon defines Tell—rather loosely, it should be added—as "a cousin of mine" and adds that "my ma [Emily] was a Sackett."[17]

Once readers of the Sackett novels accept L'Amour's words about all these cousins, they have more problems with the cousins' fathers. One exception is Lando's father Falcon. Although identified and much discussed, Falcon remains the most unreal figure in the whole saga, with the possible exception of Jubal. The father of Tell, Orrin, Tyrel, Bob, and Joe, unnamed in the fiction, left his Tennessee family for the Colorado gold fields, where he died. Echo has some brothers, but only one is named. He is Ethan, who becomes Bendigo Shafter's helper figure in *Bendigo Shafter*. Ethan explains that his father was killed by Comanches on the Santa Fe Trail when Ethan was only 14 years old. Another of Echo's brothers becomes the father of Tell et al., since L'Amour reports that Echo is their aunt.[18] Of the father of Logan and Nolan it is said only that he loved the land and is now dead. The father of Flagan and Galloway, also deceased—like most fathers of daring young men in L'Amour's fiction—left debts in Tennessee that his sons pay (*The Sky-Liners*). The forebears of Parmalee, as well as Mordecai, Macon, and Trulove, all line up shakily if at all. Since Falcon married a Kurbishaw of South Carolina, readers in the 1960s of *Lando* and *The Sackett Brand*, in both of which novels he appears, would have been correct if they had guessed that he was descended from Kin Ring. Finally, since Echo reports that she has "kinfolk down to Charleston" (*Ride River*, 2), early 1980s readers of her escapades would have been correct if they had guessed that she was related to Falcon in some manner.

Publication of *The Sackett Companion* in 1988 verified both such guesses. Readers of the Sackett novels and then *The Sackett Companion* may rightly conclude that L'Amour the novelist was exciting and teasing, whereas L'Amour the genealogist of his own dream children was also teasing, but he was inconsistent, evasive, and cocky as well.

For a writer who extols hearth and home joys, L'Amour strangely depicts no Sackett heroes settling down much to such. Tell's most poignant quest is for his father's grave far from home. Flagan and Galloway have lost their father and return home only to pay his debts. Logan and Nolan have lost their father too, but they prefer to remain apart; neither is revealed as a husband or father. Falcon when widowed left his son Lando in neighbors' hands and went treasure hunting; later father and son queasily hanker for the same woman. Parmalee is handsome and established, but he mentions no family. L'Amour wants to show male pioneers surging westward for adventure before consummation of homemaking dreams.

With other Sacketts, L'Amour played variations on his theme of adventure between old home gone and new home built. Ange Kerry is rescued by Tell in Colorado (*Sackett*), is called his wife (*The Sackett Brand*), but is not seen again, having been raped and murdered offstage. Echo's grandfather Daubeny is said to have been a woodsman, marksman, and builder in Tennessee, as well as a Revolutionary War veteran and a reader (*Ride the River*). Earlier, readers learned more about this man but without being given his first name (*The Lonely Men*). Drusilla Alvarado, a major Hispanic female in L'Amour, appears or is mentioned in eight novels. Tyrel meets her on her ancestral land in New Mexico, aids her grandfather, marries her, and takes her to Mora (*The Daybreakers*). Tell admires Drusilla (*Sackett*); but, although she is often mentioned later (*The Sackett Brand, The Sky-Liners, The Lonely Men, Treasure on the Mountain, Lonely on the Mountain,* and even the non-Sackett novel *Catlow*), nothing is said about any children she and Tye have. Flagan and Galloway rescue Judith Costello from villains in Colorado (*The Sky-Liners*); later they stand off other bad men in the Shalako region, where Maighdlin Rossiter catches Flagan's eye (*Galloway*). But L'Amour never disclosed whether either Judith or Meg ever became a mother of more Sacketts. Soon after benighted Orrin rashly weds narrow-eyed Laura Pritts, she deserts him in favor of continued loyalty to her corrupt New England father, Jonathan. The only child Laura and Orrin have exists nowhere but in the vengeful mind of depraved Laura, who sends Tell into Sonora after her imaginary "Orry" in the hope that Apaches will kill him.

Minor Sacketts abound. Macon is a Clinch Mountain ginseng picker along the Ohio River, while Mordecai is a reclusive hunter, a bit wraithlike, but Echo's rescuer by the all-too-human means of homicide. Echo calls him a cousin, but that term may mean little. Uncle Regal, her deceased father's brother, would aid the girl on her Philadelphia mission but for a recent tussle with a bear that mauled him. Trulove, an Ohio River logger, would come to her rescue but arrives with Macon, to whom he is vaguely related, only in time to tend the wounded and bury the dead (*Ride the River*). When Emily asks Logan if he is Tarbil's no-account Clinch Mountain son, the gunman replies, "Grandson, ma'am."[19] Tell reports that his "great-grandfather fought in the Revolution. He was with [Colonel Henry] Dearborn [a distant L'Amour relative (see *Frontier,* 66)] at Saratoga [1777], and he was in Dearborn's command when they marched with General [John] Sullivan to destroy the towns of the Iroquois [1779]."[20] Tell reports that his "Grandpa sailed the seas with [Stephen] Decatur and [William] Bainbridge," and (in 1804) battled Barbary pirates (*Sackett,* 2). Is this the same grandfather Tell said cut pirate Ben Mandrin's face in a sword fight off Hatteras (*Mojave Crossing*)? Flagan says in *Galloway* that one of his grandfathers lived to be 94 years old. He must have been a Sackett.

Many of the roughly 750 non-Sackett characters in the 17 novels are *personnages reparaissants,* à la Balzac. For example, Cap Rountree, wily old pal of Tell, Orrin, and Tyrel, appears in seven (*The Daybreakers, Sackett, The Sackett Brand, The Sky-Liners, Galloway, Treasure Mountain,* and *Lonely on the Mountain*). The Tinker, named Cosmo Lengro in one novel (*Lando*), figures in six (*The Sackett Brand, Mustang Man, Galloway, Ride the Dark Trail, Treasure Mountain,* and *Ride the River*). Barnabas's ally Jublain (not to be confused with Barnabas's son Jubal) appears in three (*Sackett's Land, To the Far Blue Mountains,* and *The Warrior's Path*). Many historical figures appear in prominent or minor ways. Among numerous examples may be cited Wyatt Earp and Bat Masterson (*The Sky-Liners*); Governor Edmund J. Davis of Texas (*Lando* and *Mustang Man*); Louis Riel and Alphonse Lepine (*Lonely on the Mountain*); and Al Seiber (*The Sackett Brand*).

Sack Time

The problem of dating events in the Sackett saga is often perplexing. *The Sackett Companion* is sometimes of little aid. Its glossary, called "Chronology of the Sackett Novels," imprecisely dates *Lando* ca. 1873–75 and nine narratives of allegedly later years ca. 1875–79 (331). One should not blame L'Amour unduly. In the quarter-century during which he published his 17 Sackett books, he also wrote 48 other novels and assembled much else. His memory must have been sorely tried.

Many of L'Amour's family-saga serials may be dated easily. Like Balzac, Zola, Galsworthy, and Faulkner, L'Amour sprinkles dates at key points. But again like Balzac and Faulkner, among others, L'Amour makes small mistakes or at least remains obscure.

The Sackett subset featuring Barnabas, Kin Ring, Yance, and Jubal is easy to date. *Sackett's Land* opens in 1599. *To the Far Blue Mountains* continues from 1600 to the Jamestown Massacre (22 March 1622) and a couple of years beyond that event. *Jubal Sackett,* though lacking dates and other helpful time references, takes place in the 1620s. *The Warrior's Path* mentions the year 1630 in the first chapter.

Then a two-century hiatus follows, until *Ride the River* resumes the action in 1840. In this novel Echo twice mentions that Barnabas was the clan founder. But she exaggerates when she says that every living Sackett is knowledgeable concerning the Sackett family tree back to about 1440.

Next is the subset of seven novels featuring Tell and his two most

important brothers, Orrin and Tyrel. A few hints sketch bits of action
from Kin's and Yance's time to the time of Tell et al. In *Lonely on the
Mountain* Tell recalls that "it was old Yance Sackett who began it some
two hundred years back"—"it" being the family's stock-driving "way
of life." Tell explains that Logan and Nolan were "Clinch Mountain
Sacketts, right down from ol' Yance" (5, 14). Just when might William Tell Sackett have been born? When *The Daybreakers* opens, in
1866 (in *Treasure Mountain,* Orrin explains that he and Tyrel "crossed
the plains in '66 and '67" [45]), that Tyrel is 18 years old, that Orrin
is 24, and that Tell is the oldest brother. Early in *Sackett,* Tell says that
he is 28 and four chapters later identifies the year as 1875. But from
data in *The Daybreakers* the reader may infer that Tell is at least 25 in
1866, hence 34 or more in 1875.

L'Amour places some action in *Mojave Crossing* at Cahuenga Pass,
outside Los Angeles, and says that the outlaw Tiburcio Vásquez was
recently captured there. This arrest occurred 4 May 1874. The better
for dating purposes, L'Amour says that Tell's beloved Ange Kerry
(whom he rescued in *Sackett*) is visiting relatives in the East. By the
start of *The Sackett Brand* Tell calls Ange his wife and soon thereafter
records the date of her murder—25 April 1877. The Apache leader
Victorio tends Tell's wounds in the Mogollons and sees him on his way
to Camp Verde, where Tell encounters the scout Al Seiber; both Victorio and Seiber were in this region in 1877.

Accompanying *The Lonely Men* are more time problems. Since Tell
informs his friends that Ange is dead, the time must be late 1877 and
a little after that. Next, Orrin's ex-wife Laura persuades Tell to risk his
neck in an attempt to rescue her nonexistent son. Even though Tell has
often been away from his brother Orrin, who married Laura in Mora
in 1867 but soon left her because of her disloyalty, Tell would defi-
nitely have heard that Orrin was not the father of any child by her. In
Sackett Tell visited his mother in Mora, where she was living with Tyrel
and Drusilla; the old lady would have gossiped about Laura's defection.
L'Amour cannot get off the hook by lamely having Tell comment thus
about Orrin in *The Lonely Men*: "I did recall some talk of his marrying,
but none of the details" (18). In addition, the action of *Lonely on the
Mountain* takes place in 1870, at which time Tell and Orrin ride the
range together and would have discussed Laura.

Both *Lonely on the Mountain* and *Treasure Mountain* are troublesome
as to datable action. The former reads as though it ought to be taking
place later than the time frame from *Sackett* through *The Lonely Men.*

Further, in *Lonely on the Mountain* Orrin is said to read a lot, including *Century* magazine, which was founded in 1881. This date, for a cattle drive by Sackett brothers gathering to aid their jeopardized "cousin" Logan, makes more sense than 1870, the action's exact date. Another inconsistency is Tell's recollection of the Civil War and his cattle work with real-life Nelson Story along the Bozeman Trail right after the war as occurring "a long time ago" (*Lonely Mountain,* 36). The date 1870 is exact, however, because L'Amour vivifies the Sackett cattle drive into Canada, then west of Forts Qu'Appelle, Carlton, and Garry, south of Winnipeg, through having Orrin arrested by métis leader Louis Riel's men at Fort Garry. L'Amour introduces Riel as the leader of an insurrectionary provisional government established at Fort Garry after the Hudson's Bay Company left Prince Rupert's Land and the métis began to be submerged by whites flooding in from eastern Canada. Canada took control of the region on 1 December 1869, by which time Riel had seized the fort and executed a Canadian; but being unable to solidify his gains, he sought amnesty, failed to receive it (as of 24 August 1870), and escaped into the Dakotas. L'Amour's Riel gives Orrin permission to drive his supply carts through, and the cattle drive continues into June and July—obviously in the year 1870.[21]

The dating of *Treasure Mountain* is easy, but the novel includes an error. In it Tell says that his wife Ange is gone and that he probably will not ever see again Dorset Binney (heroine of *The Lonely Men*); so the action of *Treasure Mountain* follows that of *The Lonely Men,* which is after *The Sackett Brand,* placed in 1877. Early in *Treasure Mountain* the reader is informed that the action starts in the wild New Orleans of the 1870s. So the date of *Treasure Mountain* must be 1878 or 1879. But Tell and Orrin in it undertake the mission of finding the trail of their father, long missing in the San Juan Mountains of Colorado; they iterate monotonously that the trail is 20 years old. Back in *The Day-breakers,* however, Ma Sackett reminisced in 1866 thus: "Eighteen years now I've seen you growing up, Tyrel Sackett, and for twelve of them you've been drawing and shooting. Pa told me when you was fifteen [in 1863] that he'd never seen the like."[22] So L'Amour is careless when he repeatedly writes in *Treasure Mountain* that Pa Sackett has been missing for twenty years, which would be since about 1858.

Lando is also easy to date (although L'Amour in *Companion,* 331, got it wrong). Admittedly its opening is confused. It may be in 1867 and certainly by 1868. Two explicit dates are given. They are 1869 and 19 November 1875, the latter being the day Lando escapes from the Mexican prison in which he has been confined for six years. *Lando* connects with two of the seven novels starring Tell, Orrin, and Tyrel. When Lando, in *The Sackett Brand,* hears that Tell is in trouble in the Mogollons, he quits a winning poker game and rushes to his aid. Later, Tell in *Treasure Mountain* secures fresh horses from a man who knew Lando after he got out of prison and recalls betting on his pugilistic skills in Texas.

Since Logan, narrator of *Ride the Dark Trail,* recalls rushing to help Tell in the Mogollons, in 1877, his story must take place later in the 1870s. It is not of much help for L'Amour to send Logan to Brown's Hole, where he encounters real-life Isom Dart, Tip Gault, Mexican Joe Herrara, and at least one of the Hoy boys. The activities of these notorious fellows were too extensive in time. Actually, to be truthful, Logan close to 1880 might not have found so many gunslingers in Brown's Hole as his creator would have his readers believe.

The Sky-Liners, Galloway, and *Mustang Man* are connected only tenuously to the other Sackett novels. For example, when in *The Sackett Brand* Tell calls for aid in the Mogollons in 1877, his "cousins" Flagan and Galloway rush to help. These same brothers are the heroes of both *The Sky-Liners* and *Galloway.* L'Amour dates the former by one historical aside: in Dodge City, Flagan and Galloway meet Marshal Wyatt Earp and Sheriff Bat Masterson, which places the action in 1878.[23] *Mustang Man* connects least of all with the other Sackett books. Late in it, the narrator-hero Nolan is befriended by Ollie Shaddock, the sheriff who advised Tyrel during the Sackett-Higgins feud. Ollie had also transported Ma Sackett and her youngsters out to Mora, where he wished to enter politics. But by the time of *Mustang Man* he is in the wagon-freighting business out of Santa Fe and hires Nolan in the town of Loma Parda. Early in the novel, Nolan recalls hearing a story "seven or eight years back" from a man possibly on the dodge "from the Davis police" (31). This is a reference similar to one in *Lando* concerning Governor Edmund J. Davis, whose criminal, carpetbagging police made Texas hot for good men as well as bad in 1868, 1869, and 1870. So the action of *Mustang Man* must be 1875 or so.

The Best of the Sacketts

Readers desiring a historical acquaintance with the Sacketts briefer than that provided by all the volumes completed by L'Amour may wish to know that *The Daybreakers, To the Far Blue Mountains, The Sackett*

Brand, Sackett's Land, and *Ride the Dark Trail* comprise a well-modulated quintet among the 17 Sackett volumes. *Sackett's Land* starts it all, with Barnabas leaving the socially stratified England of Queen Elizabeth and William Shakespeare for the Carolinas, with their Indians, beaches, and opportunities for adventure and trade. *To the Far Blue Mountains* shows Barnabas prospering in family and money and starting his dynasty, especially with sons Kin Ring and Yance. *The Daybreakers* is an exciting novel in its own right, though flawed in the characterization of minor figures, and it has the added advantage of first presenting some post–Civil War Sackett brothers. *The Sackett Brand* continues the exploits of Tell and shows him in anguish and full of hatred. *Ride the Dark Trail* introduces a different breed of Sackett in Logan, an outlaw, and connects the Sacketts to the Talons through Emily.

The Sackett volumes that death prevented L'Amour from writing, however, might well have become his most revealing. In *The Sackett Companion* he hints at several on the drawing board or in his head. He promised to dig out the vessel that was wrecked and half buried in the sand where Barnabas took shelter (in *Sackett's Land*) and that reappeared (in *To the Far Blue Mountains*) and to feature it "in a future book, as yet unwritten" (*Companion,* 32). He added that Jubal "will appear again, here and there" (54). He surmised that swordsman-killer Rafe Bogardus of *The Warrior's Path* "no doubt . . . will appear again in his own good time" (71). He vowed to stress Daubeny "in my book on the American Revolution" (89). He said of Tell that "the great love of his life was in his Civil War period, a tale yet to be told" (111). And he reported that Macon, Mordecai, and Trulove's "exact connection to the rest of the Sacketts is . . . yet to be revealed" (252). But L'Amour struck one sad note when he admitted that "many stories of the Sacketts remain to be told, and some may . . . remain untold" (252).

What a generation of American readers has gained from L'Amour's Sackett books is a memory of separate exciting adventures played out against a variegated backdrop of American frontier history and connected by the sturdy Sackett (i.e., American) virtues of self-reliance, courage, stoicism, loyalty, martial smarts, and dignity.

Chantrys and Talons

It is regrettable that L'Amour did not preplan his saga of his 60 or 70 main Sackett people more carefully and then write it all out with fewer interruptions. But for various reasons, no doubt partly commercial, when he was hardly halfway through with the Sacketts he began two other family serials—his Chantrys and Talons. Hints about these two families appear in three Sackett novels: *Ride the Dark Trail, To the Far Blue Mountains,* and *Ride the River.* In addition, *The Man from the Broken Hills,* which L'Amour long mislabeled a Sackett segment, links Sacketts and Talons. Clearly, then, at least as early as 1972, the date of *Ride the Dark Trail,* Chantrys and Talons were in the author's mind alongside his more fertile Sackett clan. In fact, by that time, L'Amour had already published his first Chantry offering, which is *North to the Rails* (1971). Then in 1974, he publicly announced his grand design: "Some time ago, I decided to tell the story of the American frontier through the eyes of three families—fictional families, but with true and factual experiences. The names I chose were Sackett, Chantry, and Talon. . . . Story by story, generation by generation, these families are moving westward. When the journeys are ended and the forty-odd books are completed, the reader should have a fairly true sense of what happened on the American frontier" (*Sackett's Land,* v–vi).

Making such a statement in 1974 was bold. L'Amour was then 66 years of age and had published 12 Sacketts, 2 Chantrys, and no Talons, that is, only 14 of a projected 40 or more titles. The whole project was hardly a third done, in an effective writing career starting late and already spanning more than a quarter-century. To boot, L'Amour soon sidetracked himself with *The Walking Drum,* the first volume of his announced Kerbouchard trilogy, and *Last of the Breed,* so open-ended that he rather obviously planned a sequel.

L'Amour obviously had bitten off more than he could possibly have lived to chew. In a 1981 interview he said that, besides tracing his Sackett family back to the fifteenth century and planning ten more Sackett novels, he also had ideas for at least five more Chantrys and probably five more Talons (*Comstock,* 421–22). He then described the following contrasts between his three main fictional families:

The Talons are builders primarily. They hail from Brittany. They are one way or another caught up with building. Milo Talon not so much, . . . but most of the Talons in the stories should be building, bridge construction, ships, that sort of thing. The Chantrys are better educated than the other two [families] and they're Irish and are involved in statecraft and many other things. The Sacketts are primarily frontiersmen. I've got a book planned [never published] set during the American Revolution in which I will have a Sackett on the frontier and a Chantry in the seats of the mighty, you might say. (*Comstock*, 422)

In a 1983 interview, he reiterated previous commentary and added new data concerning both the Talons and Chantrys:

The original ancestor of the Talons was a one-handed pirate, a very dangerous old man who came over here with many millions of dollars and settled in the Gaspé Peninsula in Canada. I haven't told much about him but he is one ancestor who lives on through the rest of his family. He's left his mark on all of them. The Talons become builders in the New World. Jean Talon, in *Rivers West*, for instance, is a man who builds with heavy timber. . . . He built bridges. He built churches. He built ships. He built steamboats. He built whatever there was to build. And he comes west at the time [1821] when they're building steamboats in Pittsburgh, which is the focus of my novel [not so].

Fair Blows the Wind is the story of Tatton Chantry. That isn't his real name. I never tell his real name and I never expect to tell. I'm the only one who knows. Even his wife doesn't know. But he was a descendant of Irish kings. His father was killed by the British and he had to leave Ireland in a hurry, and he takes that name. He stows away in a ship thinking he's going to France and winds up in England. Then, through a series of adventures, and a lot of sword fighting, he comes over to America. He lands over here on the coast of Carolina.

The Chantrys and Talons are allied in different points in time by marriage with the Sacketts. And their lives run parallel, especially the Sacketts and Chantrys. Very early on, individuals of the two families meet and then part and then meet again. (*Gods*, 465–66)

As noted earlier, during the year of his death L'Amour was still writing about his saga plans. One sly comment in *The Sackett Companion* relates to his Chantry-Talon sequence:

The first book of the Talon series remains to be written, though it has been started. The first of the Chantry series was FAIR BLOWS THE WIND, in which the vessel abandoned with much of its cargo of silver still aboard is the same hulk in which Barnabas Sackett takes shelter on a sandy island in the river.

When and how that silver will be discovered again remains to be told in a future story, but at least now you know the connection. It is not often I share such secrets beforehand. (245)

Although L'Amour readers know much more about his Sacketts than about his Chantrys or Talons, they are able to consult eight volumes dealing with those two families. The whole sequence begins with *Fair Blows the Wind.* In it the hero-narrator Tatton Chantry reveals that his father died at the hands of the British in Ireland ca. 1573 and left him memories of a coastal home, scholarship, gems, and swordsmanship. Tatton adds that his deceased "mother's people were of the *Tuatha De Danann,* who ruled Ireland before the coming of the Milesians."[24] Tatton takes the name Chantry from someone else. L'Amour has him comment cryptically:

Tatton Chantry . . . a borrowed name belonging to a man long dead, a man from where?

Who had he been, that first Tatton Chantry, that stranger who died?

I remembered him from my father's time, remembered the night we had lifted him from the sea, a handsome young man, scarcely more than a lad.

Dead now . . . yet living in me, who bore his name. Had he family? Friends? Estates? Was he rich or poor? Brave or a coward? How had he come where we found him?

A mystery then, and a mystery still. *(Fair Wind,* 30)

All this mumbo jumbo would seem to have more than a proper share of "Poe-esque" nonsense in it. Why the mystery? Late in *Fair Blows the Wind,* all disasters behind him and much passion spent, Tatton and his wife Guadalupe have a son back in Ireland, ca. 1590. End of that story.

Next is *The Ferguson Rifle,* which presents Ronan Chantry leaving North Carolina and then Boston for the west to hunt in the newly acquired lands of the Louisiana Purchase, ca. 1804. Such a leap from the late sixteenth century to the early nineteenth left too big a gap for L'Amour ever to have expected to fill. Anyway, next in the Chantry/ Talon saga comes *Rivers West,* which presents the earliest Talon for L'Amour fans to know. He is Jean, the muscular timber wielder, who since he starts out from the Gaspé must be a direct descendant of old Talon the Claw. Like Ronan Chantry, Jean too heads for the Louisiana Purchase. Therefore, once the fans met scholarly Owen Chantry in *Over on the Dry Side* in western Colorado in 1866,[25] they were not too surprised when the next Talon segment starred Milo, who in *Milo Talon* continues the adventurous life partly detailed in *The Man from the Broken Hills.* It should be mentioned, although L'Amour tried by interview comments to spike this objection, that for a member of a building family Milo does little to honor the tradition except to build a successful case against a scoundrel who hires him as a detective.

Then along came *Borden Chantry,* the titular hero of which, though a Chantry, is no scholar whatever. So, just like Milo Talon, he too deviates from family tradition. Nor is his son Tom likely to be very learned with respect to books and such, since the family holdings have been wiped out by adverse Colorado weather in the early 1880s and Borden, as noted, has become a law officer. Next chronologically is *North to the Rails,* which features Tom, grown up in the softer (pro-Chantry?) East, but not scholarly in any sense, and now back in the west heading up a cattle drive perhaps as late as 1890.

Other Chantry action is minimal. In *Ride the River,* 80-year-old Finian Chantry is a delightfully limned Philadelphia lawyer who aids Echo Sackett, not least by ordering his handsome, strong, but spoiled nephew Dorian Chantry to help the girl once she starts heading west again. In *Son of a Wanted Man* Borden joins law–and–order forces with Tyrel Sackett. In addition, L'Amour planned to have Finian Chantry meet another Sackett a long time ago. In *The Sackett Companion,* L'Amour reports that "Finian Chantry . . . fought in the War of the Revolution alongside Daubeny Sackett and has reason to remember the Sackett name" (87).

What gaps of decades and centuries and what illimitable expanses of geography L'Amour might have populated with more Chantrys and more Talons—to say nothing of hordes of additional Sacketts—can hardly be imagined. He said that his vast sweep of fiction, when completed, would tell the story of the ever-advancing American frontier. But he did not live to complete it. So, untouched by his magic are the times of the French and Indian War, colonial unrest, the American Revolution, and the Civil War. Still by the time he died, Louis L'Amour had manfully toiled and abundantly earned both fame and rest.

Chapter Eight
L'Amour's Style

The fiction of Louis L'Amour fulfills the first requirement of narrative literature. It is exciting. But it does not fulfill enough of the criteria of literary art. Although it reveals much about its author, holds up a mirror to an epoch, and teaches the reader something of abiding value, the age that it reflects is not L'Amour's but rather a bygone time, and his art though vivid is often flawed and cannot be called organic.

L'Amour was a best-selling anachronism. He wrote gripping melodrama, not tragedies. His heroes could be killed at any time, and this would end the adventure. But they always survive, as in happy-ending fairy tales and old-fashioned movies. His heroes are often epic questers, possessing the virtues of Ulysses, but not those of Aeneas or Dante. They use all the weapons that are at hand, including cunning, to win through to establish or reestablish a happy home, either for themselves or for others. Hence their future is never national so much as it is personal. Nor do L'Amour's characters ever learn much through suffering. They usually wind up only more sure of all they began by believing. Still, they are melodramatically heroic figures, whereas his villains, since they usually fail, fall, and learn almost nothing, are mostly absurdist characters.

"Just a Story-Teller"

L'Amour told an interviewer in 1976, "Don't put me down as a novelist, and don't say I'm an author. I'm just a story-teller, a guy with a seat by the campfire. And I want to share with people what I have found, and what I have seen, and the wonderful old voices of men and women talking of those bygone times." He went on to boast that he never plotted a story in advance. "I always write off the top of my head, although the story locale and characters have often been in mind, or partly so, for some time." Finally he added, "I go over it [the first and only draft] to correct typos. No editor has ever given me advice or suggestions. They just ask when they will get the next book" (Keith, 24:5, 8–9). Late in his life, he revealed his modus operandi, which though amateurish worked for him: "My method of telling . . . tales is simple: I place my characters in an existing situation and let it happen to them"; "Once created the characters often take on a life of their own, and often I find that I cannot leave them alone, and must return and offer a further glimpse of their lives and fortunes"; and then, "What happens after develops as a result of the personalities involved, the country itself, and the circumstances that attended their travel through it" (*Companion*, 14, 253, 241).

In *The Lonesome Gods* L'Amour has a character insist that good narrative literature should be read aloud, so as "to hear those rolling cadences . . . [,] to hear the language, to feel the sounds" (115–16). Even when he is not indulging in orotund rhythms, which he often does, his best narratives read like a storyteller's impromptu yarns. For example, one hero-narrator ends his second chapter this way: "And that was how I met Con Judy, and how we rode together on a trail that wasn't to see an end for a long, long time."[1]

L'Amour unconsciously rationalized certain stylistic faults but also highlighted his main strength, that of an old-fashioned tribal historian. The most important thing for a tribe is its ground, and L'Amour starts with that. Next come the heroes exploring and defending that ground, and in that tradition, L'Amour imbeds his best characters in their locale. He is a master of scenic description, as well as depicting action and character growing out of a specific environment.

Living Nature

L'Amour was an artist in the way he described dawns, sleepy noons, sunsets, deserts, canyons, volcanic and mountain scenes, shimmering summer, autumn foliage, winter blizzards and forest snow, verdant spring, seascapes and ocean storms, clouds, moonlight, rain, and animals in movement in their habitat. He sensibly advises his readers to study a given outdoor scene in different lights. For example: "One really never knew mountains unless he had seen them at both sunrise and sunset" (*Callaghen,* 31). When an interviewer commented to L'Amour that he "must have quite an eye for terrain," he replied, "Yes, I do. If it happened to interest me at the time, I can describe the country beside a road I was driving along 12 years ago."[2] In *The Sackett*

Companion, which often reads like a traveler's guidebook, L'Amour confides: "In writing my stories I try to present as accurate a background as possible. The stories may be fiction, the settings are not" (239).

The temptation is great to quote extensively from this author for whom "no amount of seeing ever made nature old" (*Dry Side,* 85). Sometimes the picture is impressionistic: "The sky was an impossible blue, the soft wind was chill but fresh and pleasant" (*Breed,* 61). "Trees like black bars against the gray rock. Moss hanging, moss clinging" (*Jubal,* 61). "Navajo Mountain still had a crown of gold and crimson, the gold fading, the crimson lingering" (*Mesa,* 140). Sometimes the picture is harsh: "This was my world, this barren, lonely place, this vast pink-and-copper silence, this land of dancing heat waves and cruel ridges. Here where even the stones turned black from the sun . . ." (*Gods,* 352). Often the scene is poetically rendered: "So still you could hear one aspen leaf caress another, the moon wide and white shining through the leaves, and just above the dark, somber spruce, bunched closely together, tall and still like a crowd of black-robed monks standing in prayer" (*Ride Trail,* 164). His canvas is sometimes highly detailed: "Cypress trees were festooned with veils of Spanish moss. Water oak, hickory, tupelo gum, and many other trees clustered the banks, and hummingbirds danced above the water, opalescent feathers catching the light" (*Jubal,* 98).

Setting is usually integrated with action: "The way led up a draw between low, grassy hills. Before us the land grew rough, off to our right lay a vast sweep of plains, rolling gently away to an [*sic*] horizon lost in cloud. Huge thunderheads bulked high, a tortured dark blue mass that seemed to stir and move, but flat beneath where lightning leaped earthward."[3] Many of L'Amour's nature watercolors emphasize the deterministic view that beneath a golden but indifferent sky man conducts affairs puny by comparison: "It was a pleasant day, the sun made leaf shadows on the ground around, and a few high, lazy clouds drifted in the sky. There was no violence around . . . except in that ring of silent guns, aimed at me" (*Mojave,* 145–46). Or, more tersely: "The mountains were on their right, raw, hard-edged mountains of rock thrust up from the desert floor, neither friendly or [*sic*] unfriendly, only indifferent" (*Callaghen,* 19).

When L'Amour describes western nature, he often includes animals. Here, a certain hero is traveling by railroad: "We rumbled over a bridge, slowed down for some reason, and I looked out to see the sun was down, the sky streaked with red, and a herd of antelope keeping pace with the train."[4] L'Amour's favorite animal is the horse, about which his readers can learn much in the course of reading his complete works. Tell Sackett buys three appaloosas: "One was a gray with a splash of white with black spots on the right shoulder, and a few spots freckled over the hips, black amidst the gray. The other horses were both black with splashes of white on the hips and the usual spots of the appaloosa" (*Treasure,* 55–56). L'Amour concludes that horses are faithful if trusted, are "homebodies" even when regarded as wild, and when talked to can "sense . . . the kinship of interests if no more" (*Gods,* 230, 236). More menacingly, he adds that "there are few things more terrible in battle than an infuriated mustang stallion" (*Long Hills,* 53). It is indicative of L'Amour's early enchantment with horses that his finest horseflesh appears in three early stories: Silverside, the rodeo horse in "Rowdy Rides to Glory" (reprinted in *Lonigan*); Cholo Baby, the racehorse in "Ride or Start Shootin'" (in *Long Ride Home*); and Big Red, the huge horse in "No Man's Man" (in *Long Ride Home*). A killer horse provides the name of the short story "The Ghost Maker" (in *The Outlaws of Mesquite*). L'Amour also lectures his readers on bears, cougars, dogs, mules, porcupines, wolverines, wolves, and the like, not to mention other living creatures great and small, such as bees, buzzards, eagles, and jays. Nor are flowers neglected. For example, in "Love and the Cactus Kid" (*The Outlaws of Mesquite*) the Kid spots sego lilies, lilac sunbonnets, forget-me-nots, chia, and verbena in his search for a bouquet for his girlfriend.

Characters

L'Amour populates this teeming western Eden with a variety of people in addition to rocks and plants and animals. His typical hero is broad-shouldered, thin-hipped, military in bearing (and often in experience), taciturn but capable of poetic utterance, and possessed of a philosopher's appreciation of scenes, beasts, and women. He is always a fighter—and a wild one if aroused—but he rarely throws the first punch or shoots the first bullet. He fights with fists as often as with firearms, can take enormous punishment, and retaliates with swift precision.

The first five heroes in L'Amour's long fictional works establish the major characteristics, the best figures being the titular Hondo and Kilkenny. Later heroes are better read, almost always through a program of self-education. But their most admirable virtues are neither

combat prowess nor intellectual strength. They are, rather, the ability
to adapt to nature's contours—physical, moral, and spiritual; the willingness to learn from solitude and silence, the great western teachers;
and lowlier traits such as patience, loyalty, dignity, and, once in a
while, humor.

L'Amour regarded his western heroes as Homeric. He often made
this clear, as, for example, when the father of the hero of *The Lonesome
Gods* says, "This is a day for Homer. . . . His people were very like
those around us now [Arizona, ca. 1850]. Achilles or Hector would
have done well as mountain men, and I think Jed Smith, Kit Carson,
or Hugh Glass would have been perfectly at home at the siege of Troy"
(82); and, later, "You will find that our Homers will sing of the plains,
the deserts, and the mountains. Our Trojans may appear in feathered
war bonnets, but none the less noble for them. Our Achilles may be
Jim Bowie or some other like him, our Ajax might be Davy Crockett
or Daniel Boone" (116).

L'Amour's heroines usually believe and accept that the west is
mainly male terrain, in which the best women mostly get to walk
beside (not behind) their men, while those men hold compass, map,
and weapon and point the way. His heroines are physically attractive,
often with red, red-brown, or red-gold hair and gentle hands. They are
spunky, learn to fend for and defend themselves, and generally speak
softly. Above all they are homemakers. In fact, L'Amour said repeatedly that the function of women is to make babies and homes, while
that of men is to nurture such homes in all the good ways. Typical of
a dozen such comments is one to the effect that "just as the maternal
instinct is the strongest a woman has, just so the instinct to protect is
the strongest in a man." L'Amour continues: "It was man's natural
instinct, bred from the ages before men were even men, to protect the
family."[5] And their women? "They were practical. Their very nature
as bearers of children made them so. For whenever they looked at a
man there must always be the subconscious question of whether that
man could take care of her and her children" (*Quick,* 75).

Curiously, for a writer who stresses the presence of women in the
west as he does, L'Amour was a singularly unerotic writer; in fact, he
was almost Victorian in his reticence about sexuality. Too defensively,
he tried at least twice to deflect the charge that there was little love-
making in his fiction. In 1984 he opined that "people at that time
[westerners in the nineteenth century] were more concerned with
building the world than with their sex lives. Sex is a leisure occupa-

tion, and they didn't have much leisure."[6] Liking this phraseology, he amplified it shortly before his death: "I am not writing about sex, which is a leisure activity; I am writing about men and women who were settling a new country, finding their way through a maze of difficulties, and learning to survive despite them" (*Education*, 153). So it should be no surprise to learn that there are only a dozen references even to bosoms in his fiction, half of them in *The Walking Drum*, a L'Amour novel that is exceptional in other ways as well. As late as *Jubal Sackett*, L'Amour was so reluctant to get specific that one reviewer kidded him about it: "The only bodily functions they [the characters] engage in are the chewing of jerky and the healing of wounds. As for sex, in one impassioned love scene, Jubal and Itchakomi actually hold hands in the shadows. But this is after they are married."[7]

The warmest kiss anywhere in L'Amour's fiction appears in the early story "West of the Tularosas": "He [Ward McQueen, foreman] drew her [Ruth Kermitt, his boss] to him. His lips stopped hers and he felt her body strain toward him and her lips melt softly against his. He held her there, his lips finding their way to her cheek, her ears, and her throat. After a few minutes she drew back, breathless.

'Ward! Wait!' [Ruth said]."[8]

The most electric cowboy in L'Amour's fiction is Lou Morgan, narrator-hero of "No Man's Man," another early story. If L'Amour had ever indulged in double entendre, which he did not, one might suspect him of it when he has Morgan say of Nana Maduro of Cherry Creek, "She knew how to handle men and she was used to doing that. She had been able to handle me, once. That was long ago. I'd left tracks over a lot of country since then."[9] The most aroused female in L'Amour's fiction is depicted thus: "Gretchen . . . knew she was in love with him, knew it deep in every throbbing corpuscle, knew it in her muscles and bones and in the crying need of her body, her loins yearning for the man he was."[10]

Tangentially related to heroics and love affairs, profanity and obscenity are also almost nonexistent in L'Amour's writings. There are only seven "God damn" usages, two conversations with "heck" in them, one "son-of-a . . . [*sic*]" (*Skibbereen*, 170), and one "crap" (*Proving*, 16). One villain is depicted as having "cursed obscenely."[11]

What about these villains? They upset nature itself, because they grab and despoil the land, and in the process subvert the efforts of heroic providers and homemaking heroines. Villains are also dishonorable in their mode of fighting. They hire underlings, whose vacillat-

ing loyalty is bought rather than earned. They shoot from ambush.
They tell lies. When the hero lies, it is for a good cause and hence is
justifiable; and often the hero is up-front in his announcement of strategy, if not tactics. But when the villain lies, he does so to spread "evil"
(an old-fashioned word common in L'Amour) and hence deserves the
reader's opprobrium. L'Amour's blackest villains are those who seek to
dishonor women—for example, Colonel Ashford, who is in the white-
slavery business in *The Shadow Riders,* and would-be rapist Gomez in
Jubal Sackett.

Structure

It would be too much to expect that L'Amour, given his haphazard
style of composition, would craft novels having much architectural
symmetry. He is more like a hasty impressionistic painter, leaving
spots of canvas almost bare but loading on the color at points of em-
phasis, or like a romantic musical composer whose work has unbal-
anced parts but whose emotions are true and crashing.

L'Amour is best with openings and endings. "Hit your reader on the
chin. So he knows he's in a story. The reader doesn't want to know
what's *going* to happen. He want[s] to know what's happening *now.*
You've got to get the reader in the first two minutes." L'Amour so
advised a writing conference audience in 1967 (Keith, 24:8). This
statement mocks the device of foreshadowing and implies that the best
way to sustain reader interest is by creating serial climaxes.

A L'Amour opening may be an awakening, a mystery, trouble, or a
tragedy. "A brutal kick in the ribs jolted him from a sound sleep and
he lunged to his feet."[12] "He lay sprawled upon the concrete pavement
of the alley in the darkening stain of his own blood, a man I had never
seen before . . ."[13] "It was Indian country, and when our wheel busted,
none of them [other wagon-train members] would stop."[14] "Smoke
lifted from the charred timbers where once the house had stood" (*Valley
War,* 1).

After the beginning, however, L'Amour often encounters some difficulties in his storytelling. One of his most besetting midnovel problems is false foreshadowing. Of a hundred examples, here is a simple
one. The lawman in *Borden Chantry* says of the unknown murderer,
"I'm never going to quit until we get this man in jail."[15] But this
promise is never fulfilled. L'Amour planted both foreshadowing sign-

posts and misleading path markers on his fictive terrain, because he did not know in advance how his plots would turn out; and, as he often boasted, he never rewrote.

Another of L'Amour's problematic stylistic devices is his alternation of first-person limited narrative point of view with omniscient point of view, which is sometimes stimulating but often simply confusing, especially when sloppily done. At best, it results in heightened interest in the reader, in a sense of superiority over the leading participants, and in authorial irony. But sometimes the switch from limited to omniscient point of view is wrenchingly sudden. In more than one novel, the ventriloquial author forgets which voice he is using. For example, on three occasions in *Ride the River* L'Amour calls Echo Sackett, who is his narrator through much of the action, "she" (107, 114, 179), when "she" should be "I." Three times on one page of *Lonely on the Mountain* narrator Tell Sackett is called "he" (188).

Such weaknesses aside, one of L'Amour's most adroit plot mechanisms is his cinematic vectoring of action lines. A splendid example may be found in chapter 18 of *The High Graders,* in which the hero starts with his crew over a ridge with mules carrying gold, which the villain—followed by a secondary villain, who alerts the hero's turncoat friend—aims to intercept; meanwhile, a crony of the main villain rides by with the kidnapped heroine, paralleling the hero's route. Akin to this converging of activities in a narrative is the plot pivot, that is, a sudden dramatic swing in the direction of the action. For example, a character may suddenly make a dramatic announcement: "Kilkenny, I want you to kill my son!"[16]

Too often, however, when L'Amour rushes his action toward the climax with much "vectoring" and "pivoting," he marshals events with a comic-strip reductiveness. Note, for one example among dozens, the jammed-up action in the penultimate chapter of *Reilly's Luck,* during which the hero is busy ruining the villain at poker just when the villainess's gunman is closing in on that hero. The narrator-hero of *The Lonesome Gods* says toward the end of his struggle against natural forces, evil men, ignorance, prejudice, and the demands of love, "It all was falling together at last" (433). Such a statement describes many of L'Amour's simplistic finales.

L'Amour advised neophyte writers of fiction to point every stylistic and plot ingredient toward the end, and then sign off with "a smile, a laugh, or a chuckle."[17] He often follows this advice himself, but sometimes the chuckle gets smothered by an incredulous gasp. Consider, as instances, the closures of *Kilrone* (a corpse), *The Cherokee Trail* (a scalping), and *Last of the Breed* (a deadly promise).

Words

L'Amour built his quickly constructed books with about six million words. Although his vocabulary is primarily a rather basic English, he does achieve precision of diction; in addition, his word hoard is enriched by many foreign and some technical words, western localisms, certain significantly repeated key words, and crisp similes and metaphors.

L'Amour loved many aspects of scientific study, especially concerning western geology and horticulture. Therefore, innumerable scientific terms come into play in his works. The following are imbedded in a single page of the mining novel *Comstock Lode*: quartz, calcite, galena, pyrite, argentite, and sphalerite (131). But it seems inappropriate when Tell Sackett, the wise but only semiliterate narrator of six Sackett novels, spouts complex geological lingo, as he occasionally does. For example, in *The Lonely Men* he pauses to discuss, between colloquial barrages, "faulted" earth, "quartz veins," "cretaceous bed[s]," "diorite," and "dikes that intruded" (166).[18]

Key words in L'Amour, often in clusters, include *accept, almighty* (as an intensive), *bait of food, evil, eyes, fate, field of fire, good, home, hunch* (or *feeling, instinct, notion, sixth sense*), *lie* (i.e., "recline," often in a wrong grammatical form), *listen, lonely, loyal, patience, responsibility, shoulders, silence, stand, trouble, water,* and *will* (noun).

Taken together and studied, these words help the reader to picture the author (not simply his narrators) as speaking colloquially, being concerned with raw good and evil, not believing totally in fate but in will power as well, being overly conscious of broad-built and observant men, being respectful of basics, being aware of manifold dangers, and living in awe of western silence.

Action radiates from many of these words, like heat from a campfire. L'Amour admired the concentrated activity of big, strong men fighting "evil." One of his most energetic heroes ponders thus: "He felt no animosity toward anyone, nor any desire to do evil. Yet, did evil men ever think of themselves as evil?"[19] The implicit, far-off goal of almost every L'Amour hero is to find a home. Early in *Jubal Sackett*, in which the word *home* appears more than 20 times, the hero locates a beautiful spot in the west, calls it "a quiet, secluded, lovely place!," adds that "this would be my home," and toward the end of his narrative states, "I had found my home" (79, 288). Like all good westerners, L'Amour's sensible characters trust their hunches. The author best defines "hunch" in this passage: "The mind gathers its grain in all fields, storing it against a time of need, then suddenly it bursts into awareness, which men call inspiration or second sight or a gift" (*Drum,* 421). Being lonely was a given for people in the underpopulated west of the nineteenth century; hence the word *lonely* is also a common one in L'Amour. Loyalty, patience, and a sense of responsibility are cardinal American virtues, often recently more honored in the breach than in the observance. But they are, perhaps for that very reason, common elements in the typical L'Amour hero and heroine, as basic as blood and bone.

Poetic Prose

Having first published as a poet (though a poor one), L'Amour naturally enough employed many similes and a fair number of metaphors in his prose, which is also sometimes poetically rhythmic. Like a good westerner, he used images from poker more than from any other category. Most such tropes are routine, but here is a special one. Covered from doorway and window by rifles, one clever hero shows a pair of puns, saying, "I never draw against a full house" (*Tucker,* 68).

The four most common images in L'Amour's fiction describe rain as a mesh of metal, creek water as chuckling, stars as lamps, and stealthy movement as ghostlike. The crispest image in all of L'Amour may well be contained in this refreshing notion, often repeated: "The air was fresh and cool, so much so it was like drinking water from a spring just to breathe it."[20] Sunsets and trees evoke some of L'Amour's finest figurative effects. Here are four examples from among scores: "The sky was shot with flaming arrows that slowly faded, leaving a kiss of crimson on the edges of the clouds, and the prairie itself turned a sullen red, darkening into shadows and the night" (*Ferguson,* 21); "The sentinel pines stood straight and dark, austere as nuns at prayer" (*Dry Side,* 158); "Snow . . . banked the trees to their icy necks" (*Jubal,* 225); and "Directly before him, there was a grove of wild, wind-torn trees looking like a clutch of hags with their wild hair blowing in the wind" (*Breed,* 291). The following metaphor describes all of L'Amour's heroes, half his heroines, and L'Amour himself: "I thought of them then, those four young men who rode with me, four young men carved from the . . . oak of trouble" (*Gods,* 341).

Akin to imagery in L'Amour is his occasional, very effective use of an almost scannably rhythmic prose. It is especially noticeable in *The Ferguson Rifle, To the Far Blue Mountains, Fair Blows the Wind, The Warrior's Path, Jubal Sackett,* and *Last of the Breed.* Examples: "No other rides with me, and the plains lie vast about" (*Ferguson,* 1); "Green lay the coast and gray the sea"[21]; and "Cold was the day when finally it came," and "Long they talked as the night drew on and her father slept" (*Breed,* 224, 251). Such basic rhythms when enhanced by alliteration are doubly appealing, as in "dust devils danced upon the desert's face" (*Valley War,* 124), or "deep were the depths into which it descended."[22]

Humor

Most western writers are humorous. L'Amour is almost an exception. Perhaps his grasp on western history was too serious. When he made up for lost time and tried to strike a comic tone, as in the otherwise hopeless novel *Fallon,* he could be momentarily effective. The cocky young narrator of "What Gold Does to a Man" (reprinted in *Buckskin Run*) and the folksy narrator of "The Nester and the Piute" (reprinted in *Riding for the Brand*) quickly establish their comic voices and sustain them well to the end, although the latter trivializes violence in the process. In addition, L'Amour's seriously challenged heroes make humorous asides. For example, when the heroine of *Jubal Sackett* tells the hero that she is "a Sun [Indian princess] of the Natchee," he replies," I am Jubal Sackett, a son of Barnabas" (130). It seems legitimate (if amusing) to conclude that his characters, even his first-person narrators, can be funny while L'Amour himself was not a very humorous man.

Chapter 6 of *Matagorda* has an amusing sequence of comic range talk by cowboys around a herd. *Chancy, Conagher, Where the Long Grass Blows,* and *Milo Talon,* among a few other works, feature a good deal of humorous lingo, much of it deriving from guns, danger, and death. Not much comic language in L'Amour concerns sex. So one must make the most of what is available: "That Claire girl . . . can cook, too!" ("That Triggernometry Tenderfoot," *Long Ride,* 56.) "But you've got to admit she keeps what she's got so you know it's there" (*Mojave,* 102– 103). "He was jumping around like mad [boiling coffee had been thrown in his lap] and I could see I'd ruined his social life for some time to come" (*Ride Trail,* 33). And "that girl . . . busted a pretty little dent in the ground when she hit stern first" (*Sky-Liners,* 14). Sometimes L'Amour's humor sounds traditionally Southwestern, with typical exaggeration and deadpan delivery. Thus: "He was so thin he would have to stand twice in the same place to make a shadow"[23]; "There were men came into that place so rough they wore their clothes out from the inside first" (*Lonely Men,* 28); and, "He was a gnarled and wizened old man with a face that looked old enough to have worn out two bodies" (*Noon,* 149). But the prize line of humor in all of L'Amour comes when a bunch of cowpokes are discussing Shakespeare: "Garry took a gulp of coffee. 'That Shakespeare, now, I think he *borrowed* a lot here and there. Why, ever' once in a while I'd come on things in his plays that I'd heard folks sayin' for years. All he did was write them down.'"[24]

So Shakespeare is full of laughter-generating clichés? Well, so is L'Amour. Sometimes he takes them and adapts them for humorous purposes, as with "he would fight at the drop of a hat, and drop it himself" (often repeated), "Don't beat . . . around the greasewood,"[25] or dozens of other adaptations. Unfortunately, L'Amour often pulled out his verbal chestnuts without injecting any variation to ensure freshness. Some of these phrases are merely western conversational neutralities, such as "shot to doll rags," "light a shuck," "brassy sky," "bite the bullet," "hold the fort," and "he's a man to ride the river with." Just as often, L'Amour too hastily settled for nonwestern clichés instead of striving for something new. This was probably an inevitable result of the speed with which he composed and published. Examples among a hundred include "that doesn't cut any ice" or "that doesn't cut the mustard," "up a tree" or "up the creek without a paddle," "not on your tintype," "little pitchers have big ears," "rub him out," "the fat is in the fire," "a wild-goose chase," or—L'Amour's favorite—"I'll tear down your meathouse." (Admittedly, a majority of these hackneyed lines appear in L'Amour's dialogue, where an ordinary, unoriginal effect most probably was often intentional.)[26]

Little Errors

It may have been forgivable, in the name of fabulous sales figures, for L'Amour to employ a few hundred quick clichés instead of slowly striving for more memorable effects. But his compositional errors, though rarely serious, are another matter altogether. After all, the man boasted ad nauseam of being self-educated and of never being taught to write, and he even advised his readers that a program of private study could educate them as thoroughly as fireside perusal of Plutarch and Blackstone tutored some of his imaginary bronco-busters. But the truth is that L'Amour's books are loaded with just about every common error pointed out in basic writing courses.[27] L'Amour could have profited from basic freshman English instruction. It may well be true, as he repeatedly preached, that "many . . . teachers know nothing" (*Proving*, 108) and that "there is no real way in which one writer can help another" (*Education*, 114). However, most novelists and English teachers are aware of the following sorts of compositional errors. Since L'Amour evidently never was, he could have used a little help. Because of space limitations, only the most blatant bloopers are briefly quoted.

Antecedent disagreement: "Each person is alone within their minds."[28] The word *centered* misused: "hopes center around" (*Sackett's Land*, 53). "Cannot help but . . ." Dangling modifiers: "Crawling in, there was room . . . Walking on, night came" (*Gods*, 91), and "Flying over, it was just one more narrow place" (*Breed*, 259).[29] The phrases "due to" and "equally as" misused. *Further* for *farther*: "He would find the right place somewhere farther on, and from that point he would go no further."[30] "Kind of a" and "sort of a." *Lay* for *lie*, etc.: "I . . . laid back and shivered" (*Jubal*, 175). "Not un-": "A pueblo not unlike those near Taos" and "thick paper, not unlike papyrus" (*Mesa*, 258, 293). Number errors: "one of the things that has protected me" (*Lost Creek*, 121). Parallelism violated: "He was either looking for the hideout or he was stalking somebody" (*Breed*, 107); and "The man . . . had either been there . . . or he had met with her somewhere" (*Mesa*, 111). Pronoun misuse: "a foreign thing to we of England" (*Blue Mountains*, 218); "a good place for Keokotah and I" (*Jubal*, 135); "like she herself" (*Breed*, 269); "like an oyster who rests" (*Gods*, 32); "to we"[31]; "the lips the sigh sent I" (*Smoke*, 63); "whom I now knew had joined him."[32] "Reason is because" (*Outlaws*, 85, 142). Squinting modifier: "the sister who painted occasionally sold something" (*Education*, 152). *That* clauses used to introduce sentences: "That Wulff was being given furs he did not doubt. That he might overlook a few things . . . was also probable. That he would in any way betray his government Zamatev did not believe" (*Breed*, 123). *That* doubled: "It was obvious to him that even if they did kill the gringo that it would do nothing" ("Long Ride Home," *Long Ride*, 157). "Try and." And what may be called "x and that y": "They said I had no choice. Some men had been murdered and that I would also be killed" (*Milo,* 128).

L'Amour also makes substantive mistakes, such as renaming a given character or place, miscounting animals or wounds or corpses, getting the year wrong, and the like. Typos are another source of annoyance to the reader. For one example among more than a thousand in L'Amour's published books, *coolly* is mispelled as *cooly* nine times in *Where the Long Grass Blows.* There are more than a dozen typos and punctuation oddities in *Bendigo Shafter,* more than a score in *Fair Blows the Wind,* and almost 40 in *Riding for the Brand* (2 each on pages viii, 109, and 114).

L'Amour, however, despite his errors and infelicities, which range from the gross to the minuscule, may still quite properly be esteemed as the most popular western writer who ever lived.

Chapter Nine
L'Amour's Message

L'Amour's message to his untold millions of readers is simple. Load up an inquisitive mind in a muscular body. Read the classics. Also, get into western American history. And above all, defend the endangered American virtues of vigorous patriotism. His works dramatize the values of fighting for family, home, region, country, and the old frontier way of life. Hence L'Amour remains more a bracing entertainer than an epic spokesman for a nation, as he tended to define himself. His fans find him comfortable to like. His work reinforces their extravagant notion that in it the fading American way of life—nothing less than the dramatic destiny of a westering people—has been presented with justifiable pride.

Books

L'Amour delighted in informing his readers that his ill-schooled heroes and heroines gained instant wisdom by reading in their spare time. For example, in *To Tame a Land* a well-read older man gives his surrogate son, the narrator-hero, a book, saying, "Read it five times. You'll like it better each time. It's some stories about great men, and more great men have read this book than any other." The book is Plutarch, which by chapter 4 the narrator says he is reading for the fourth time. By chapter 10 he reports, "Only four, so far. But I'll get to it" (18, 84). Eight chapters later he distracts the book giver, by now his enemy, with the confession that he has still read the book only four times, then kills him. (Plutarch should feel honored.) In *The Daybreakers* Orrin Sackett is taught to read and write by Tom Sunday, is inspired by stories of Davy Crockett and Andrew Jackson (who, though illiterate into manhood, succeeded in politics), impresses Tom later by remarking that he likes Charles Dickens, and still later is remembered by his brother Tell: "Orrin had started early to reading law, packing a copy of Blackstone in his saddlebags and reading whenever there was time" (*Treasure Mountain*, 9–10). [1]

The novel in which L'Amour cites the most books is *Bendigo Shafter*. In this story, Ruth Macken carries a 50-volume library west of the Dakotas. It includes items by William Bartram, William Blackstone, Timothy Dwight, Josiah Gregg, David Hume, Washington Irving, Nelson Lee, Lewis and Clark, John Locke, John Stuart Mill, Montaigne, Plutarch, Thoreau,[2] and Tocqueville. Also mentioned as part of Bendigo's spare-time reading are Charles Barras, Dion Boucicault, Bulwer-Lytton, Bret Harte, Juvenal, Anna Cora Mowatt, Hawthorne, Poe, and Shakespeare. Another bookish book is *Reilly's Luck*. Its hero Val reads Berkeley, Robert Burton, Lord Byron, Goethe, Hume, Charles Kingsley, Locke, John Gibson Lockhart, Plato, Sir Walter Scott, Spinoza, Tennyson, the Comte de Volney, and Voltaire. Burton's *Anatomy* literally saves Val's life: when a villain fires at the hero, he happens to be turning from a bookshelf with Burton's thick tome in his hand, and it stops the bullets. Killing his enemy, Val jokes, "I was never able to get through this book myself."[3]

How many of these classics did L'Amour "get through" himself? By all odds, he is the most bookish of all popular western writers. But the fact remains that most of the writers he names in his fiction, as well as most of the ones he ticks off in his *Education of a Wandering Man,* are not the titans of literature, many of whom he mentions only in passing. He never makes substantive or symbolic use in his fiction of the contents of any author either he or his characters mention. The authors who truly influenced him were short-story craftsmen. L'Amour once recalled that after getting a few hundred rejection slips for stories about boxing, football, rodeos, and history, he suddenly wondered why: "When none of them [the stories] were selling, I decided all the editors wouldn't be crazy; something had to be wrong with what I was doing. So I got a half-dozen stories by O. Henry, de Maupassant, Robert Louis Stevenson, and others I liked . . . and I went over them very carefully, step-by-step, to see what they were doing that I wasn't doing. Shortly after that I began to sell" ("The West," 6).

Western History

L'Amour is a didactic author. He offers his readers facts, both well-known and trivial, and opinions on an astonishing variety of subjects. He makes it a habit to pause in his storytelling to present informational asides, to tender advice, and to generalize. In doing so, he discusses history, frontier survival, pragmatic philosophy, love, family life, and much else.[4]

A fuller and more specific list of the subjects of L'Amour's digressions would include animals, anthropology, army life, clothes, the East, echoes, education, extrasensory phenomena, fighting, geology, gypsies, hotels, hunting, Indians, Madeira wine, the Middle East and the Far East, moccasins, nail making, patrons in Elizabethan England, sailing, saloons, Siberia, slavery (worldwide), soldiering, transportation, underwater salvage, weapons, the weather, and, above all, western life.

The subject L'Amour most enjoyed telling his readers about is western American history. In his nonfictional *Frontier,* he discusses early voyagers to and explorers of the New World, colonists on the Eastern seaboard and far inland, intrepid pioneers, primitive and early settlements, Indians, mining efforts, and gunmen. One reviewer rightly calls *Frontier* "an impressive work of expertly crafted essays," while another says that in them L'Amour "evokes the pioneer experience of the country's many frontiers."[5] Most of L'Amour's fiction may be placed and dated to a degree. Sometimes a particular scene has a real mountain, river, trail, fort, or town in it, and hence it is locatable on any detailed map. Often the action rushes forward against a historical backdrop sketched in with a few brush strokes. Always, L'Amour concentrates on his fictional characters and their activities. And always, his successful formula permits the inclusion in the background of geographical and historical reality (see *Companion,* 189, 239). One of his most effective "lessons" comes during a pause in the action of *Over on the Dry Side,* during which Owen Chantry lectures not only the attentive reader but also the ironically inattentive narrator about Ute Indians in the region and Navajos nearby, the latter's migratory habits eight centuries before (perhaps L'Amour was already thinking ahead to *The Haunted Mesa*), and Indian ghost houses by the shelf of the Mesa Verde, with the Sleeping Ute Mountains against the distant horizon.[6]

Another nice touch in L'Amour is his identifying early explorers of various regions. In his beloved Southwest they are usually Spaniards. Tell Sackett mentions Father Silvestre Escalante and Fernando Rivera, reports finding a Spanish grave in Ute country, and adds that perhaps he "was the first to see that grave in three hundred years" (*Sackett,* 17).[7] Other long-gone explorers include northern European travelers, mostly British. L'Amour honors local characters by making them repositories of historical lore, as when one old-timer warns a tenderfoot heading farther west: "Don't envy you, young feller. . . . You got a long road to travel. . . . Oh, there's folks done it! [John] Palliser done it, the Earl of Southesk, he done it, and . . . folks like David Thompson, Alexander Henry, and the like" (*Lonely Mountain,* 55).

Fort after fort, small towns, buildings therein, and western cities once rowdy and gaudy but now tame—all come under L'Amour's scrutiny and emerge vivified on his pages. What distinguishes L'Amour from most other writers of western fiction may well be the historical verisimilitude with which he presents his locales, both natural and man-made. Another, however, may be his awkward manner of handling western outlaws. For one ineffective example, the reader is treated to the following thoughts allegedly running through the mind of Kilkenny as he enters a town to clean it up: "Riding in was going to be much easier than getting out. None knew him here, to be awed by his reputation. Anyway, the old days were passing. One heard little of Ben Thompson or King Fisher. Billy the Kid had been killed by Pat Garrett, Virgil Earp had killed Billy Brooks. Names of men once mighty in the west were sliding into the grave or into oblivion" (*Valley War,* 21).

L'Amour is at his best in using real-life characters when he does it casually, as, for example, in the brief appearances of Wyatt Earp and Bat Masterson in *The Sky-Liners.* When L'Amour tries to fictionalize an important western historical personality in detail, he fails—as with Cullen Baker, hero of *The First Fast Draw.*[8]

Indians

The most vital and controversial western subjects in all of L'Amour's books are Indians, women, and the west as a microcosm of conservative America.

A monograph could be written on L'Amour and the Indian. A three-pronged thesis in it might be that Indians are both good and bad, like other branches of the human family; that their way of life has given Indians a set of values often at variance with those of white men and women; and that since the beginning of human history, migrations of people have occurred, and, therefore, the Indians of the American west could call the land theirs only so long as they could successfully defend it against intruders. L'Amour maintained these tenets through half a hundred fictional works, and his reasoning is always tough and logical; but he derives much of it from nineteenth-century sources, not twentieth-century ones. He is therefore regarded as ultraconservative, anathema to modern revisionists, and yet for those very reasons all the more popular with his mass readership. L'Amour, like other conservative western novelists before him, replicates what one critic calls "the Darwinian social philosophy [Zane] Grey used to support his portrayal of Western life."[9]

Typifying L'Amour's attitude are two statements (often adumbrated). The first is in the form of a speech by a veteran to a tenderfoot: "Ma'am, . . . Injuns are folks. They're like you an' me. . . . Some you can trust; some you can't. There's just as many honest folks among Injuns as among white or black. An' there's just as many thieves and liars."[10] The second is directly from L'Amour: "The Indians the white man met were no more the original inhabitants of the country than were the Normans and Saxons the original inhabitants of England. Other peoples had come and gone before" (*Mesa*, 19).

L'Amour often pauses to lecture thus on Indians or have a knowledgeable character do so. The best such little essays appear in *High Lonesome* and *Bendigo Shafter*, and they are echoed in *The Sackett Companion*. In *High Lonesome*, a canny old frontiersman explains that from the start the Indian was a warrior—with a cultural background at odds with that of the whites, with nonwhite behavioral standards, without mercy, enjoying horse stealing, hunting, and mortal combat, amused by torture, impressed by courage, puzzled by the weapons and persistence of whites, and indifferent to seizing territory for the purpose of holding it.[11] In *Bendigo Shafter* the hero explains to Horace Greeley in New York, when queried about "the Indian situation," that nothing can be done to avoid trouble with the Indians, whom he says most western whites compare to the buffalo, that is, "simply . . . an obstacle to settlement of the land" (261); he then expatiates on Indian hunting, war, horse stealing, failure at trade, and contempt for manual labor and on the radical differences in Indian and white religions, customs, life-styles, and value systems.

Employing his usual technique, L'Amour scatters little comments on Indians throughout much of his fiction. These notes seem to be illustrations of certain historical (i.e., "white") ideas about Indians rather than pieces of real information to be taken seriously. Most are gross generalizations that, among other things, do not recognize differences in customs and character among tribes and individuals. For example, L'Amour asserts that Indians avoid fighting to the last man, do not scare easily, do not kill camp visitors, and use "torture, not only to bring suffering to an enemy, but to test how much he could stand."[12] L'Amour further states that Indians have "superstitions" often based on good sense, believe "in medicine, or as some say, magic" (*Jubal*, 4), treat children well, respect the land, endure hunger stoically, and strive for prestige. L'Amour often discusses prehistoric Indians, comparing them as trail makers "to the merchant caravans of the Middle Ages" (*Tucker*, 24). L'Amour suggests, as did many earlier commentators, that "the death of the red man's way came when the first white trader came among them to trade what the Indian could not himself make. . . . The needle, the steel knife blade, the gun and gunpowder, the whiskey, and the various ornaments. These were the seeds of his destruction, and what he warred against was the desire in his own heart. There were those who protested against using the white man's things, but . . . no ear listened" (*Bendigo*, 95). L'Amour also voices the often-repeated line that certain "fierce and warlike . . . horse-trading Indians . . . were the finest light cavalry . . . ever seen" (*Companion*, 78).

Women

L'Amour's running commentary on women in the west is provocatively conservative and inconsistent. The topic might well be the subject of a long and valuable essay.[13] Overall, L'Amour's comments on women are a familiar mixture of flattery and denigration, attributing to women pride and saintly strength on the one hand, and manipulativeness and a desire to restrict the freedom of men on the other. The following examples are typical: "Give me always a woman with pride, and pride of being a woman" (*Warrior*, 164); "Who knows what iron is in the heart of a woman?" (*Gods*, 432); "A man, he's got to get along mostly with hard work an' persistence, but with a woman it is mostly maneuver" (*Ride River*, 94); and "Men prefer to wander and women to keep them close" (*Jubal*, 219).

L'Amour equated feminine beauty with sex appeal, but not always in a positive way. Note the implications of this statement: "Despite her obvious beauty there was . . . a certain elusive charm that prevented the lips from being sensual" (*Lost Creek*, 71). Thus he seems to say that beauty and sensuality are one thing, and charm and goodness (by implication) are quite another—the old "bad girl/good girl" dichotomy again.

For better or worse, every woman needs a man, L'Amour informed the world repeatedly. So much the better if that man is light-hearted, for "a girl can always make do with a man who smiles from the heart" (*Cherokee,* 83). Women can smile from the heart too: "No woman objects to a man looking the fool once in a while."[14] Still, "it's a bad thing for a man to be shamed in front of his womenfolks."[15]

L'Amour's men see the battle between the sexes as having a couple of predictable outcomes. "'S the way with women . . . Fall for a man, then set out to change him. Soon's they got him changed they don't like him no more" ("Love and the Cactus Kid," *Outlaws,* 32). "Gals like the high-spirited, high-headed kind [of men] . . . If they can break them to harness they aren't at all what the gal wanted in the beginning, and if she can't break them they usually break her. But that's the way of it" (*Galloway,* 54). Turning that last metaphor around, some L'Amour men suggest that obstreperous women must be handled like fractious horses (*Daybreakers,* 153; *Shalako,* 15), while one otherwise admirable hero even says that he likes the idea of polygamy (*Shalako,* 120). The theme of men as victims and women as cunning manipulators, however, is by far the most prevalent. "You know's well as I do if a woman sets her cap for a man he ain't got a chance. Only if he runs. That's all!"[16] And this: "He had seen her kind before—the ones who handled men the best because they lacked passion themselves. They were always thinking while a man was merely feeling."[17]

L'Amour's heroes, once "caught," then expect unquestioning loyalty and complete compliance from the women. "If a woman loved a man she would live [with him] anywhere" (*Taggart,* 148). Also, "if you marry him and want to be happy, you will have to grow with him" (*Valley War,* 170). Here is a L'Amouresque role model for women: "She did not ask questions, but did what he suggested" (*Noon,* 131). In L'Amour's world, women who are disloyal to their men are in for embarrassment, as the endings of "The Ghost Maker" and "No Rest for the Wicked" (both reprinted in *The Outlaws of Mesquite*) make terrifyingly clear.

The rest of L'Amour's pronouncements concerning women, especially in the west, may be disposed of with blessed brevity. The author says in many places that women could travel safely in the west, because of the high regard in which western men held them.[18] But in other places he says, contradicting himself, that women had to be protected—and not merely from natural dangers either, but also from bad men, who if they turned to molestation were quickly hanged, at least. L'Amour also says that women are easily scared—and when so should not be trusted to make decisions. But at other times he believes that they often can be trusted to handle adverse news with courage and dignity. In the opinion of L'Amour and his heroes, women are inclined to gossip and otherwise make trouble. "They're mostly in trouble, an' when they ain't, they're gettin' other folks into it," as one old hunter notes (*Ferguson,* 134). Nevertheless, L'Amour and his heroes value certain nurturing characteristics they attribute to women: their gentle hands, their usefulness at sick beds, and their ability to ease the pain of a dying man. In L'Amour's depiction of one "pleasant-looking, attractive woman," he refreshingly appeals to old-fashioned values: "Had someone asked her what she was, she would have said, 'housewife,' and been proud of it" (*Marshal,* 107).[19]

In his fiction, L'Amour's ideal woman appears to be Ruth Macken of *Bendigo Shafter,* who, the narrator-hero says, "had set a standard of womanhood against which every woman I later was to know would be unconsciously measured. She was quietly beautiful, moving with an easy grace and confidence. She was tolerant, understanding, and intelligent, a good listener ready with apt comment; she understood. . . . She had style" (300). Indisputably, L'Amour was here writing about his beloved wife Kathy, of whom he once said, "She's the perfect wife. . . . She is beautiful . . . , intelligent, reads a lot and is always busy. . . . She has a sharp business mind. She has many interests, principally her home, her children and me" (Keith, 24:9).

General Advice

L'Amour was in the habit of stopping his narrative action to offer not only information on a thousand topics but also advice on basic rugged human behavior and glacial generalizations on life itself.

He was informative about outdoor living and the tools and weapons necessary for survival there. He also lectured, sometimes gratuitously but often excitingly, on building campfires, boxing, wrestling, stabbing, shooting, tracking, outguessing the criminal mind, methods of guerrilla and allied warfare, the treatment of wounds, the dangers of wealth, fear, hatred, bravery, parenting, education, ideals, loneliness, mutability, inevitable aging, and time. He also intermittently says beware, ye softening Americans of our crisis-riddled epoch.

Here are several of L'Amour's generalizations from two thousand or so scattered through his works. Often they are spoken by fictional characters, who, however, seem usually to speak for L'Amour himself.

Sometimes these maxims are helpful; occasionally they creak or crack under scrutiny. Their dogmatism and their contents say much about L'Amour. "We do not own the land. . . . We hold it in trust for tomorrow."[20] "Fear is not a bad thing. It is fear that saves men's lives . . . It prepares them for trouble" (*Taggart*, 48). "When evil takes up to violence, the good have no choice but to defend themselves" (*Woman Creek*, 94). "Crazy ideas had a way of succeeding, because they were unexpected," and "peace was an illusory thing" (*Breed*, 16, 28). "Liquor never solves any problems, nor did it make a problem more simple" (*Kiowa*, 18). "Many troubles removed themselves if one merely waited," but also, "The way to face trouble . . . was to meet it head-on" (*Kilrone*, 135; *Brionne*, 95). "All [criminals] were incurable optimists" (*Broken Gun*, 95); then again, "most criminals are optimists" (*Passin'*, 155). "Gold is easier found than kept" (*Treasure*, 114). "And there is perhaps no one hated more by a man than one to whom he has done an injustice" (*Callaghen*, 38). "Who was altogether honest?" (*Skibbereen*, 101). "Maybe a man shouldn't have it [wealth] when he's young. It robs him of something, gives him all he can have when he's too young to know what he's got" (*Broken Hills*, 187); furthermore, "possessions can rob one of freedom just as much as the bars of a cage" (*Breed*, 241); and, "truth's a luxury the old can afford" ("The Sixth Shotgun," in *Outlaws*, 184). "In wisdom there is often pain" (*Blue Mountains*, 214). "Regret is a vain thing" (*Fair Wind*, 200). "Many look but do not see" (*Bendigo*, 140). "It is . . . as sinful not to believe in the devil as not to believe in God!" "All men can fail, and each man must somewhere find his master, with whatever strength, whatever weapon." "Many are slaves . . . who do not realize they are . . ." "There must be law . . . Man must have order, and evil must be restrained or punished" (*Warrior*, 28, 36, 64, 90–91). "There is something about a really beautiful woman that throws a man off" (*Passin'*, 9); but "all too often the man a girl thinks she loves or the girl a man believes he loves is just in their imaginations" (*Milo*, 139). "Nothing was ever gained by lying but the risk of more lies" (*Milo*, 159). One final L'Amour pronunciamento is that "the strongest . . . is he who stands alone" (*Cherokee*, 75), repeated as follows: "One is strongest when one is alone" (*Jubal*, 84).

Since L'Amour was an intensely self-conscious, self-aggrandizing writer, it is reasonable to conclude that he often generalized with the intention of projecting a flattering image of himself. Sometimes, however, the result was an image of himself quite different from what he must have intended. What is more valuable in the following generalizations than the picture that develops from them of the author himself?

"Our schools and general thinking are cluttered with beliefs long proved absurd by contemporary knowledge"; "to know a little arouses a hunger to know more"; and "no man of knowledge was ever content with what he knew" (*Mesa,* 175, 176, 183). "Wealth is important only to the small of mind" (*Hondo,* 78), and "it mattered little how much money a man had as long as he was contented."[21] "He was, as are many self-made men, curiously self-centered" (*Canyon,* 53); and "he carried himself with that impatient arrogance toward others that is often possessed by men who have succeeded by their own efforts, and too easily" (*Brand,* 135). Also "the tough ones . . . survive" because "mostly a person learns to succeed by simply overcoming failure" (*Passin',* 135, 187); still, "when a man attains great success, people are forever coming to him with ideas" (*Mesa,* 61), and "success corrodes" (*Galloway,* 117). "Sometimes I think the further a man gets from the simple basic needs the less happy he is"[22]; and "man needs so little, . . . yet he begins wanting so much" (*Breed,* 223). "Writing is a lonely business . . ." (*Fair Wind,* 154); "the ones who wind up on top are usually those with the most efficiency" (*Tucker,* 24); and "no matter how good you are, you can always get better" (*Mesa,* 131). "The trail is the thing, not the end of the trail" (*Ride Trail,* 44). Finally, "to talk too much is always a fault" (*Jubal,* 19).

Ultimately much of L'Amour's writing may be seen as pointing to the conclusion imbedded in the following dialogue. Barnabas Sackett, the narrator, and Abigail Tempany are about to be married.

She looked up at me. "Why! You're laughing!"
"It is a fault I have. There is something about solemn occasions that always stirs my humor. I like them, I respect them, but sometimes I think we all take ourselves too seriously."
"You don't think marriage is serious?"
"Of course I do. It is the ultimate test of maturity." (*Blue Mountains,* 138)

The good-humored maturity of Louis Dearborn L'Amour (né La-Moore) evolved out of a humble adolescence, a rollicking knockabout youth marked by jobs in various fields and aboard many ships, global war, and decades of intense writing—writing that is surely best when it is about the American west. L'Amour knew its past, its people, and its geography. He was happiest at work, meeting countless devoted readers of his melodramatic fiction, with friends in California and Colorado, and above all with his family at home. Thus his special knowledge and love of the west and western life enabled L'Amour to create more than a hundred books of fiction that have already given great pleasure to innumerable readers and will continue to do so for years to come.

Notes and References

Chapter 1

1. *Education of a Wandering Man* (New York: Bantam Books, 1990), 133–34; hereafter cited in text as *Education*.

2. For LaMoore family information, I rely mainly on four sources. (1) Edna LaMoore Waldo, L'Amour's older sister, whose unpublished and unpaged manuscripts (at the Alfred Dickey Library, Jamestown, North Dakota)—"LaMoore Family Background: 1862–1863, 1882" (hereafter cited in text as "LaMoore Family"); "Edna LaMoore Waldo: Jamestown, 1893: Memories, and a Varied Career Started There"; and "Parker LaMoore: 1897–1954"—are detailed and vigorously written, and whose 40 letters to me, dating from 27 June 1984 to 17 July 1990, contain unique and valuable information (hereafter cited in text as ELW to RLG, with date or dates). (2) James Smorada and Lois Forrest, eds., *Century of Stories: Jamestown and Stutsman County* (Jamestown, N. Dak., Fort Seward Historical Society, 1983), is a tribute by Jamestown residents and friends to a distinguished pioneering community; hereafter cited in text as *Century*. (3) A document titled "Scrapbook" assembled by Reese Hawkins in two unpaged binders and containing L'Amour material, including letters from, to, and about L'Amour; Hawkins, a friend of L'Amour, deposited the scrapbook at the Dickey Library, Jamestown (hereafter cited in text as "Scrapbook"). (4) Discussions my wife, Maureen Dowd Gale, and I had with several people in Jamestown, 3 and 4 June 1984.

3. Barbara A. Bannon, "Louis L'Amour," *Publishers Weekly* 204 (8 October 1973):56; hereafter cited in text as Bannon. L'Amour later softened his contention, thus: "Shortly after my wife and I were married, I was glancing over some of her family history and it immediately became apparent that our families must have known each other at several times in the past" (*The Sackett Companion* [New York: Bantam Books, 1988], 11; hereafter cited in text as *Companion*).

4. Mrs. Waldo writes that Louis and Katherine L'Amour's ancestors probably never lived in "the same small town" (ELW to RLG, 18 February 1990). Not content merely to write the sagas of intertwined westering families, L'Amour also saw himself as the common man's encyclopedia of the west and as an expert on six thousand years of history (Hank Nuwer, "Louis L'Amour: Range Writer," *Country Gentleman* 130 [Spring 1979]:99; hereafter cited in text as Nuwer; Suzy Kalter, "Louis L'Amour: He Tells How the West Was Really Won," *Family Weekly*, 10 June 1979, 7; hereafter cited in text as Kalter.) The Talon family was originally to be named Sigourney ("Research,

World-Wide Experience Grist for Mill of Frontier Author," *North Dakota Motorist*, March–April 1972, 4).

5. The L'Moore (also spelled "Larmour") family had been Huguenot refugees in Ireland before migrating to Ontario (ELW to RLG, 2 February 1990, 15 March 1990).

6. Candace Klaschus, "Louis L'Amour: The Writer as Teacher," Ph.D. dissertation, University of New Mexico, 34; hereafter cited in text as Klaschus. *See also* Waldo, "LaMoore Family"; *Century*, 52–54; ELW to RLG, 4 August 1988, 18 February 1990, 15 March 1990.

7. L'Amour dedicated *Kiowa Trail* to "Lieut. Ambrose Freeman, my great-grandfather, who lost his scalp to the Sioux, Dakota Territory, 1863" (*Kiowa Trail* [New York: Bantam Books, 1964]; hereafter cited in text as *Kiowa*). Freeman figures offstage in L'Amour's book *Taggart* (New York: Bantam, 1959), 17; hereafter cited in text as *Taggart*. The 1862 massacre is mentioned in *Callaghen* (New York: Bantam, 1972), 119–20; hereafter cited in text and below as *Callaghen*. L'Amour touches on Sibley and Freeman in *Companion*, 203. As early as 1958, L'Amour began promising Jamestown correspondents that he would write a book on the 1862 Little Crow Massacre in Minnesota and General H. H. Sibley's 1863 reprisal expedition into the Dakotas. The book was never written. Mrs. Waldo insists that L'Amour could never have written such a book, for several reasons. For one, she claimed the Sibley story was hers, because she had covered it in her memoir entitled *Yet She Follows: The Story of Betty Freeman* (Bismarck, N. Dak.: Capital Publishing Co., 1931) and in her *Dakota* (Bismarck, N. Dak.: Capital Publishing Co., 1932; rev. ed., Caldwell, Idaho: Caxton Printers, 1936). She also had control over unpublished material about Sibley and Freeman, and she owned a rare official history book that was given to Freeman and other Minnesota veterans of the Civil War and of Indian wars and to which L'Amour had no access. Furthermore, L'Amour knew no Freeman kinfolk (ELW to RLG, 9 January 1986, 15 March 1990). For years, the Sibley subject was a bone of contention between L'Amour and his sister. In 1955, he dedicated *Guns of the Timberlands* to her, spelling her maiden name, however, "Lamoore."

8. Elizabeth Freeman is the subject of Waldo's *Yet She Follows* and figures in her pamphlet *The Sunbonnet Trail* (Minot, N. Dak.: Dakota State Journal, 1946), which features a picture of this loyal pioneer wife and mother on page 4.

9. Had L'Amour lived to narrate it, his fictional character Tell Sackett's Civil War career would have been patterned partly on Abraham Dearborn's. *See* L'Amour's "Booty for a Bad Man," 1960, reprinted in *War Party* (New York: Bantam Books, 1975).

10. Edna LaMoore graduated from Jamestown College in 1914, taught in North Dakota schools, married Frank Harwood Waldo in 1920, wrote news features and reviews of western books from the late 1920s, conducted her own

popular KFYR Bismarck radio show called "Western Romancing" (reviews, interviews, etc.) 1935–37, was widowed in 1949, worked at the Stanford Research Institute (Palo Alto) as files supervisor, and now lives in Danville, California. She has been a writer and lecturer. She is the author, in addition to books already mentioned, of *From Travois to Iron Rail* (New York: B. Ackerman, 1944) and other works (ELW to RLG, 27 June 1984, 8 July 1984, 9 July 1984). Parker LaMoore was a veteran of World War I and World War II and a journalist and political writer in Oklahoma, Ohio, and Washington, D.C., for the Scripps-Howard newspapers. Late in World War II, he became an aide in China to General Patrick Jay Hurley, who was ambassador there and whose biography he wrote, titled *"Pat" Hurley: The Story of an American* (New York: Brewer, Warren, Putnam, 1932) (Waldo, "LaMoore Family"). Yale LaMoore quit high school during World War I to join the army, served in France, contracted pneumonia and diphtheria there, was never completely healthy thereafter, but returned to finish high school and attend college. He worked in Jamestown and Minot. During World War II he was an employee in management at a plant in Grand Island, Nebraska, making bombs and shells. After the war, he worked as a quality-control engineer making shells at the same plant. He died in Grand Island of lung cancer shortly after the deaths at his home there of his father and then his mother, both of whom Yale had taken care of there since 1947 (Waldo, "LaMoore Family"; ELW to RLG, 23 July 1984; letter from Yale LaMoore's daughter Annabelle LaMoore (Mrs. Rodney S.) Shindo of Omaha, Nebraska, to me, 6 November 1990; hereafter cited in text as ALS to RLG, with date). Emmy Lou LaMoore was a teenage poet (letter from Annabelle LaMoore Shindo, to me, 9 August 1984; ELW to RLG, 25 October 1989). A final LaMoore family member was John Otto, a New York City orphan sent west on an "orphan train" arriving in Jamestown 24 April 1914. John was informally adopted by Doc LaMoore and his wife, accompanied them to Oklahoma, later went to California, and may later have been killed in an automobile accident (*Century,* 54, 160; Klaschus, 12). Mrs. Waldo informs me that Otto "was almost a year older" than L'Amour (ELW to RLG, 18 February 1990). Ann Shindo recalls that her father Yale and her Uncle Louis always regarded Otto as "a family member" (ALS to RLG, 6 November 1990).

11. Arturo F. Gonzalez, "Writing High in the Bestseller Saddle," *Writer's Digest* 60 (December 1980):23–24 (hereafter cited in text as Gonzalez); Donald Dale Jackson, "World's Fastest Literary Gun: Louis L'Amour," *Smithsonian,* May 1987, 158 (hereafter cited in text as Jackson). L'Amour once wrote a friend that he concealed his age to be more influential with young readers ("Scrapbook"). Perhaps it was vanity. His literary career took off only with *Hondo,* published when he was 45. He always looked younger than his years and vitally energetic, even in his 1988 dust-jacket photographs. Mrs. Waldo writes that L'Amour was unwilling to admit his age even to his wife,

"very sternly ordered" no family reminiscing in front of her, and avoided applying for a driver's license because doing so would reveal his age (ELW to RLG, 9 September 1984).

12. It seems that L'Amour's father was a man of almost limitless energy and talents; in addition to everything already listed, he built a house for himself and his family in Jamestown. (About 1950 it was moved to another site, 402 8th Ave. SE.)

13. Mrs. Waldo writes that L'Amour did not believe he needed school and did not respect teachers (ELW to RLG, 25 October 1989) and that he "disliked school discipline" (ELG to RLG, 18 February 1990).

14. Mrs. Waldo denies this figure, saying that the total was "barely 100," since the house lacked room for more (ELW to RLG, 18 February 1990).

15. *See also* John G. Hubbell, "Louis L'Amour—Storyteller of the Wild West," *Reader's Digest,* July 1980, 96 (hereafter cited in text as Hubbell); Michael T. Marsden, "A Conversation with Louis L'Amour," *Journal of American Culture* 2 (Winter 1980):648; Edwin McDowell, "Behind the Best Sellers," *New York Times Book Review,* 22 March 1981, 34; Sandra Widener, "The Untold Stories of Louis L'Amour: The West's Best-Selling Writer," *Post Empire Magazine* (Denver), 31 February 1983, 10 (hereafter cited in text as Widener); Klaschus, 13, 67; Shirley Lee, "Louis L'Amour and the Writers of the Purple Sage," *Collectibles Illustrated* 3 (January–February 1984):50 (hereafter cited in text as Lee). Reese Hawkins says in "Louis L'Amour," *North Dakota Horizons* 5 (Spring 1975):14 (hereafter cited in text as Hawkins), that L'Amour "always had with him [during his years of wandering] copies of some of the series of little Blue Books published by Haldeman Julius of Gerard, Kansas. These sold for five to ten cents each." L'Amour describes his introduction to Blue Books as occurring when he was hoboing out of El Paso and recalls, "Often in the years following, I carried ten or fifteen of them in my pockets, reading when I could" (*Education,* 10). It would seem that L'Amour was naive in persistently trying to create a legend out of himself when he contended, as he often did, that he read 8 to 10 books at a time, read a 100 books a year intensely, scanned another 400 a year, habitually read current issues of about 30 magazines, and examined 15,000 books to select his 9,000-volume library (Kalter, 7; Gonzalez, 23; Lee, 50; *Education,* 145). "About the Author" blurbs in 1983 revealed that L'Amour's "library holds more than twenty thousand volumes" (*Hills of Homicide* [New York: Bantam, 1983], 247; *Law of the Desert Born* [New York: Bantam, 1983], 246). By 1988, the L'Amour library had slimmed down to "ten thousand selected books" which, however, were "the means of reproducing much of our civilization" (*Education,* 120). But according to the section called "About Louis L'Amour" in *The Outlaws of Mesquite* (New York: Bantam, 1990), 201 (hereafter cited in text as *Outlaws*), and in

The Rustlers of West Fork (New York: Bantam, 1991), 261 (hereafter cited in text as *Rustlers*), the library was up again to 17,000 volumes.

16. Mrs. Waldo writes that there was no financial crisis in the family, as L'Amour repeatedly implied, but that their father simply did what many families did in the 1920s—sought better conditions in the west. She adds that it was a mistake for their parents to "detour" into Oklahoma, and that L'Amour, who accompanied them, left their brother's home without saying goodbye. Mrs. Waldo also maintains that L'Amour then and later took advantage of Parker's Oklahoma home and contacts (ELW to RLG, 15 March 1990) and that Parker rescued L'Amour "from several 'jams'" there (ELW to RLG, 9 September 1984).

17. L'Amour "packed but one change of clothes and a dozen books to take to the road" (Nuwer, 99). In *Education,* L'Amour provides few details about his family during this period. He mentions accompanying his parents from Oregon to Oklahoma in their car (the unnamed year was 1931) and adds, "My intention was to see my parents settled and then go on to New Orleans and the sea" (123); but he admits that neighbors thought he "should be out rustling for a job instead of staying at home" reading books by various authors, 20 of whom he names (128–9). Mrs. Waldo writes that L'Amour often visited his parents, who lived in Oregon from the late 1920s to 1931, that they returned to Oklahoma, this time living 1931–37 in a home owned by Parker, and that they lived thereafter with Yale in his Grand Island home. Mrs. Waldo adds that "everybody helped Louis" (ELW to RLG, 25 October 1989), that he "turned up regularly at the Choctaw place . . . made it his [headquarters] for years," and that because "he did *not* correspond with me, I knew his wanderings only through our mother—and she was never quite *sure* where he was" (ELW to RLG, 18 February 1990). Mrs. Waldo quotes "our father's plaint": "'Why the hell doesn't he [L'Amour] get a job?'" (ELW to RTG, 15 March 1990). Mrs. Waldo concludes: "Louis had for years been a source of grief to our parents—exasperation to my brothers" (ELW to RLG, 9 September 1984).

18. Harold E. Hinds, Jr., "Mexican and Mexican-American Images in the Western Novels of Louis L'Amour," *Latin American Literary Review* 5 (Spring–Summer 1977):129–30; hereafter cited in text as Hinds.

19. Harold Keith adds that as a seaman L'Amour went around the world in 5½ months ("Louis L'Amour: Man of the West," *Roundup* 23 [December 1975]:4; hereafter cited in text as Keith, 23). Hawkins reports that L'Amour "was awarded 4 Bronze Stars . . . during World War II" (Hawkins, 16), which decorations L'Amour also mentions (*Education,* 159). Mrs. Waldo writes that her brother did not wish to enter military service, felt that the war would interfere with his literary career, and did not participate in the D-Day landings (ELW to RLG, 23 July 1984, 7 February 1989).

20. The only two autobiographical episodes narrated in detail in *Education* concern L'Amour's doing mine assessment and caretaking work north of Phoenix and later being stranded in the Mojave Desert and having to walk out (47–54, 65–72, 88). Mrs. Waldo writes that during L'Amour's mine-caretaking work, which was about the year 1928, their parents were in nearby Kingman, Arizona, and provided him help, "as usual" (ELW to RLG, 4 July 1984). This counters L'Amour's often-repeated assertion of juvenile self-reliance—for example, "I was never helped by anyone" (*Education,* 180). Mrs. Waldo also contends (ELW to RLG, 3 July 1984) that she insisted upon her brother's telling Bantam filler writers to stop including his ridiculous claim that he was "a descendant of François René, Vicompte [*sic*] de Chateaubriand, noted French writer, statesman, and epicure" (*Guns of the Timberlands* [New York: Bantam, 1955], 149 [hereafter cited in text as *Guns*]; *Sackett* [New York: Bantam, 1961], 152 [hereafter cited in text as *Sackett*]).

21. Wesley Laing, "Introduction" to Louis L'Amour, *Kilkenny* (Boston: Gregg Press, 1980): xi; Louis L'Amour, "Of Guns & Gunmen," *Gun World* 25 (September 1984):54–56. L'Amour avers that he qualified in the army as an expert with six different types of firearms ("Scrapbook"); see also *Education,* 35–36.

22. Mrs. Waldo writes that before his marriage L'Amour "dated some exotic women, none of them 'settled'" (ELW to RLG, 15 March 1990). L'Amour's niece Ann Shindo adds that "in his letters, Louis wrote about stories he was working on, girls he dated, books he'd read and encouraged us to read" (ALS to RLG, 6 November 1990).

23. The name change distressed his sister, especially when it resulted in her own old name being confused with his new one (Waldo, "LaMoore Family"; *Century,* 54). To add to the confusion, in L'Amour's book *Education* under Doc LaMoore's picture (128–29) are the words "My father, Dr. L. C. La Moore (he altered the spelling)." L'Amour concludes the poem "In Protest," in *Smoke from This Altar,* rev. ed. (New York: Bantam, 1990), as follows: "I am hot on the spoor / Of all who fail to say L'Amour / Which is my name" (56). This 1990 edition is hereafter cited in text as *Smoke.*

24. *Smoke from This Altar* (Oklahoma City: Lusk Publishing Co., 1939; rev. ed., New York: Bantam, 1990), originally contained 36 poems, usually short, including 15 Italian sonnets. The best poems sketch elements of nature so stormy, mountainous, and oceanic that they dwarf petty man; the worst delineate a persona who cannot be held back by transient love but must ever wander. In 1990 Bantam reissued *Smoke from This Altar,* with an introduction by L'Amour's widow, Kathy L'Amour, and a supplement entitled "Newly Collected Poems," 20 in number. The book is beautifully printed but a bit overpriced, and the new poems add nothing to L'Amour's reputation as a poet. Mrs. L'Amour's introduction is poignant as reminiscence but valueless as biography or criticism.

25. L'Amour's son Beau L'Amour, in an Afterword to *The Rustlers of West Fork,* writes a good deal of nonsense about his father's denial for "thirty-eight years" (247) that he ever wrote 4 novels under the pen name Tex Burns and quotes his casuistical explanation: "I just wrote them for hire. They weren't my books" (248). For decades now, bibliographers have given Tex Burns as a L'Amour pen name. Interestingly, the L'Amour Trust now sees no objection to capitalizing on Tex Burns's efforts, despite L'Amour's denigration of them all in this sweeping statement: "Beau, . . . I don't care for the books" (248). Of his other pen name, L'Amour reports, "I had written a series about Asia for the pulps about a character named Ponga Jim Mayo. The publisher at Standard Magazines did not believe people would buy westerns written by anyone with my name, so they wanted something 'western sounding,' whatever that is. So I pulled Jim Mayo out of the hat" ("Western Writer Will Be Honored," *North Dakota Motorist,* March–April 1972, 4). Ponga Jim Mayo is the derring-do hero of 7 stories reprinted by L'Amour in *West from Singapore* (New York: Bantam Books, 1987); hereafter cited in text as *Singapore.* In one story, "South of Suez," Mayo in the course of a few hours is knifed in the shoulder underwater by a villain whom he then kills, is knocked unconscious by repeated head blows, escapes from a snake pit, is stabbed by another villain whom he knocks cold and carries to a crevice and drops to his death, and only thereafter removes the knife from his own ribs. No wonder L'Amour wanted to be Jim Mayo.

26. See John D. Nesbitt, "Louis L'Amour's Pseudonymous Works," *Paperback Quarterly* 3 (Fall 1980): 3–4.

27. This excellent story was reprinted in *War Party* and again in *Reader's Digest,* September 1984, 102–106.

28. See "Merchandising," *Publishers Weekly* 164 (21 November 1953): 2120.

29. L'Amour, "The West—The Greatest Story Ever Told," *Roundup* 27 (July–August 1981):6; hereafter cited in text as L'Amour, "The West." The sum was later reported to be $5,000 (Mei-Mei Chan, "Louis L'Amour: The Fastest Pen in the West," *USA Today Weekend,* 30 May–1 June 1986, 4; hereafter cited in text as Chan).

30. Tom Rogers, "Author Louis L'Amour Surveys His Range," *USA Today,* 29 March 1983, 4D; hereafter cited in text as Rogers.

31. These figures have been compiled mostly from paperback-cover and dust-jacket publicity. Garry Abrams, in "L'Amour's Legacy," *Los Angeles Times,* 17 November 1989, E12, paraphrases L'Amour's Bantam editor to the effect that "about 220 million copies of L'Amour works—mainly paperbacks—have come off the presses over the decades." The dust jacket of *The Rustlers of West Fork* quotes the figure as of 1991 to be "225 million."

32. "Bantam Announces Its Plans for the Louis L'Amour Overland Express," *Publishers Weekly* 217 (9 May 1980):36. Someone once remarked that

the most valuable book in New York after L'Amour had been through seeking publicity was any book he wrote but did not autograph (Robert Phillips, *Louis L'Amour: His Life and Trials* [New York: Knightsbridge, 1990], 150; hereafter cited in text as Phillips).

33. "L'Amour, Louis (Dearborn)," in *Current Biography* (New York: H. W. Wilson Co., 1980), 204; Jon Tuska and Vicki Piekarski, eds., *Encyclopedia of Frontier and Western Fiction* (New York: McGraw-Hill, 1983), 211; Brian Garfield, *Western Film: A Complete Guide* (New York: Rawson, 1982), passim.

34. The National Library of Spain, in Madrid, catalogues 29 translations of L'Amour's works.

35. Richard S. Wheeler, "Anomie and the Western," *Roundup Quarterly* n.s. 2 (Spring 1990):17. However, Wheeler complains in "Writing the Realistic Western Novel," *Writer* 103 (October 1990):20, that L'Amour "so dominated the field for so many years" that he "was both an asset and [a] liability to the western story." Wheeler also criticizes L'Amour's inability to characterize in depth.

36. "Scrapbook"; "Louis L'Amour, Jamestown Native, Remembers Kin in Book Dedications," *North Dakota Motorist,* March–April 1972 (hereafter cited in text as "Jamestown Native"); Nuwer, 102; Jack Evans, "Louis L'Amour: The Boy from North Dakota Who Made It Big . . . Biggest . . . in the Book Writing Business," *ND REC Magazine,* July 1981, 15 (hereafter cited in text as Evans, "L'Amour: The Boy from North Dakota"); Widener, 12. L'Amour had a movie agent but no literary agent (Jackson, 162). Mrs. Waldo is convinced that marriage to Kathy "*made* Louis L'Amour," since she encouraged him to settle down, keep regular hours, and thus become more productive; moreover, she applied to their financial affairs a "business ability" "evidently inherited . . . [from] her father . . ." (while availing herself as well of his commercial and legal connections), and L'Amour was able to benefit from her range of personal and Hollywood friends, including Alan Ladd, his wife, and their family (ELW to RLG, 9 September 1984, 15 March 1990). L'Amour dedicated *The Broken Gun* to Ladd and his sidekick William Bendix, both having died two years earlier.

37. "Scrapbook"; "Jamestown Native," 4; Nuwer, 102; Evans, "L'Amour: The Boy from North Dakota," 12.

38. "Scrapbook;" J. D. Reed, "The Homer of the Oater," *Time,* 1 December 1980, 107 (hereafter cited in text as Reed); Frances Ring, "An Interview with Louis L'Amour," *American West* 19 (July–August 1982):48 (hereafter cited in text as Ring); Lee, 50.

39. *See also* Ned Smith, "He's No Rhinestone Cowboy," *American Airways,* April 1976, 12.

40. *See also* Jon Tuska, ed., *The American West in Fiction* (New York and Scarborough, Ontario: New American Library, 1982), 229; hereafter cited in text as Tuska.

41. *See also* Jack Evans, "Authenticity in Stories Has Made L'Amour Great," *Jamestown Sun,* 1 December 1978, 11; and Louis L'Amour, "Foreword" to *The Sackett Novels of Louis L'Amour,* 4 vols. (New York: Bantam, 1980), 4:vii. This 1980 set is obviously incomplete, despite its title.

42. Tim Cahill, "The Land and Louis L'Amour," *Outlook,* February–March 1982, 29 (quoted in Klaschus, 196).

43. *See* "Louis L'Amour Sues Carroll & Graf," *Publishers Weekly* 224 (8 July 1983):20–21; John Mutter, "Judge Curbs C & G's Use of L'Amour's Short Stories," *Publishers Weekly* 226 (22 July 1983):65; Leonore Fleischer, "Black Hats, White Hats," *Publishers Weekly* 226 (5 August 1983):101.

44. Also, in *Riding for the Brand,* there are so many errors in composition and proofreading that the book is a publisher's disgrace, obviously issued fast for profit only. *Night over the Solomons* and *West from Singapore* are similar slapdash profit-making collections of early war and sea yarns, plus introductions. L'Amour so valued his essay on mercenaries in the former that he repeated three paragraphs of it verbatim in a later introductory essay in the same book (*Night over the Solomons* [New York: Bantam Books, 1986], 44, 125; hereafter cited in text as *Solomons*).

45. *Shalako* (New York: Bantam, 1962), 17; hereafter cited in text as *Shalako*. *See also* "Novelist to Build Frontier Village," *North Dakota Motorist,* March–April 1972, 5.

46. 2 August 1982, *Congressional Record,* 97th Congress, 2nd sess., H4934-H4937, and 12 August 1982, *Congressional Record,* 97th Congress, 2nd sess., S10402. *See also* "L'Amour Receives Congressional Medal," *Publishers Weekly* 224 (14 October 1983):17. Retired Los Angeles and Jamestown journalist Jack Evans, long a L'Amour friend, fan, and commentator, was primarily responsible for L'Amour's getting this award. Starting in 1978 he wrote and mailed more than three thousand personal letters, at his own expense, to catalyze interest among L'Amour's readers and ask them to urge their congressional representatives to nominate him for the medal.

47. "People," *Time,* 23 August 1982, 61.

48. *New York Times,* 27 March 1984, A25; and Jory Sherman, "Along Publishers Row," *Roundup* 32 (May 1984):27.

49. Mrs. Waldo informs me that L'Amour's son "produced the cassettes and some films" (ELW to RLG, 28 March 1990).

50. *The Trail of Memories: The Quotations of Louis L'Amour,* compiled by Angelique L'Amour (New York: Bantam, 1988); hereafter cited below as *Trail of Memories.* Its 11-week best-seller status attests only to the loyalty of L'Amour's fans.

51. *See* James Barron, "Author Louis L'Amour Dies at 80; Chronicler of the American West," *New York Times,* 13 June 1988, D12; Phillips, 197; "Remarks upon an Honorary Doctor of Literature Degree Awarded Posthumously to Louis L'Amour by Bowling Green State University on November 4, 1988," *Journal of Popular Culture* 23 (Winter 1989):190.

52. L'Amour said, "I never smoked" (*Education,* 95; *see also* Phillips, 196). Also, the theory about his illness proposed in his obituary is not very plausible, because his mining experiences were only brief episodes when he was in his twenties (*Education,* 47–54). Mrs. Waldo has noted, however, that the L'Amour home in air-polluted Los Angeles is near heavy Sunset Boulevard traffic, that their grandfather Abraham Dearborn had chronic asthma, and that their brother Yale died of lung cancer (ELW to RLG, 15 March 1990). As for L'Amour and alcohol, he has an early autobiographical character wish that he had "beer in ponds" (*Smoke,* 48), while in his posthumously published autobiography he writes both that "I . . . rarely had a drink" and later that "I was never a drinker" (*Education,* 95, 172).

53. The first mention I have seen of L'Amour's "autobiography" appeared in 1983: "His publisher wants him to write his autobiography. Louis doesn't think he wants to. He hesitates a bit, trying to explain why. 'I don't like to sit here overweight, in a place where I can go up and get a damn good meal if I want to, and a good bed to sleep in. I'm not sure I could recapture the way I was or the way I thought. . . . It's hard to get those feelings back again, because I don't feel that way anymore'" (Widener, 10). L'Amour may strike some readers as charming here, but he is really being doubly uncandid. His fiction shows that he can recapture feelings of deprivation, and he loved to write and talk about himself. Further, he wrote me on 18 January 1984 that he was then in the midst of composing a two-volume autobiography and that he did not want me to interfere by publishing any extensive biographical material about him. Mrs. Waldo writes more than once that she doubted her brother ever would or even could write an accurate autobiography, since he freely mixed memory and imagination in dealing with his past. In one letter, Mrs. Waldo states that L'Amour untruthfully claimed that their grandfather Abraham Dearborn told him stories about the Civil War, that Indians visited their Jamestown home, and that their father lost money in North Dakota banks and left the state during the Depression; she concludes "that he [L'Amour] *deliberately* confuses the dates and facts of his career" (ELW to RLG, 9 September 1984). It is also L'Amour's niece Ann Shindo's opinion that "he never would've written an autobiography" (ALS to RLG, 6 November 1990).

54. ELW to RLG, 1 October 1984.

Chapter 2

1. In *Education,* 96–97, L'Amour touches on violence in literature—in fairy tales, the Bible, and the works of Shakespeare—and in the horseplay of boys, then adds that "in my . . . stories, there is no violence for the sake of violence. I tell it as it happened and my books are all thoroughly grounded in history." He concludes that "many of us who abhor violence often forget . . . that we have peace and civilized lives because there were men and women who went before us who were willing to fight for our freedom to live

in peace" and that "violence is with us still, and no one is immune to a sudden strike in the night" (97).

2. Polti's book, *Les trente-six situations dramatiques* (Paris, 1895), was translated by Lucille Ray as *The Thirty-Six Dramatic Situations* (Boston: Writer, 1916).

3. Frank Gruber, *Pulp Jungle* (Los Angeles: Sherbourne Press, 1967), 184–86.

4. John G. Cawelti, *The Six-Gun Mystique* (Bowling Green, Ohio: Bowling Green State University Press, 1971), 35–67; hereafter cited in text as Cawelti. Cawelti expanded *The Six-Gun Mystique,* which does not discuss L'Amour, into part of *Adventure, Mystery, and Romance: Formula Stories as Art and Popular Culture* (Chicago and London: University of Chicago Press, 1976), which does discuss him, though somewhat inaccurately: "A western novel written by Louis L'Amour in the 1960s is somewhat franker and more graphic [than in the 1950s] in the portrayal of sex [not true] and violence [not true], and . . . more ambiguous about the moral qualities of its hero [not true]" (231). Incidentally, the most violent fiction L'Amour ever wrote is reprinted in *West from Singapore.*

5. Mrs. Waldo writes that she "probably" read the manuscript of "'Drum' . . . as long ago as 1966–67" (ELW to RLG, 1 October 1984).

6. *The Haunted Mesa* (New York: Bantam, 1988), 104; hereafter cited in text as *Mesa.*

Chapter 3

1. L'Amour in 1977 said that there are no "ethnic villains" in his fiction (Hinds, 133). He must have forgotten Don Pedro in "Long Ride Home," reprinted in *Long Ride Home,* and Chico Cruz of *The Daybreakers.* (Villainous Don Isidro in *The Lonesome Gods* would come later.) L'Amour made partial amends by having Don Pedro die honorably and by later saying that Chico Cruz had "a streak of madness in him" (*Companion,* 102).

2. Matt says that "the advantage of academic education is somewhat overrated" and concludes that Pearson should have avoided a military career and instead "should have been teaching in a grade school or the floor walker in a department store" (*Westward the Tide* [New York: Bantam, 1977], 28, 214).

3. Loren D. Estleman notes "parallels" between *Hondo* and the earlier novel *Shane,* by Jack Schaefer; see *The Wister Trace: Classic Novels of the American Frontier* (Ottawa, Ill.: Jameson Books, 1987), 42; hereafter cited in text as Estleman.

4. Introduction to *Hondo* (Boston: Gregg Press, 1978), ix, viii. John D. Nesbitt, in "A New Look at Two Popular Western Classics," *South Dakota Review* 18 (Spring 1980):36–39, suggests that Hondo, like his dog Sam, is rough, dominant, fast, and free, while Angie, like a good horse, is tamable

and must learn to obey her western man. Nesbitt notes that Hondo's and Angie's hearth will be on his ranch in California, not on hers in Arizona.

5. Introduction to *Utah Blaine* (Boston: Gregg Press, 1980), v–ix.

6. *See* L'Amour's letter to Wesley Laing, after the latter's introduction to *Kilkenny* (Boston: Gregg Press, 1980), xi.

7. Foreword to *The Rider of the Ruby Hills* (New York: Bantam, 1986), viii.

8. Keith Jarrod, Introduction to *Crossfire Trail* (Boston: Gregg Press, 1980), v–vi.

9. Love at first sight is also presented in "Showdown on the Tumbling T," reprinted in *The Outlaws of Mesquite*.

10. *Last Stand at Papago Wells* (New York: Bantam, 1986), 2, 49.

11. *Sitka* (New York: Bantam, 1957), 41.

12. L'Amour made good use of historical sources and poetic license in depicting Sitka. When the Russian flag was lowered a final time there, it was fouled and cut down during a misty evening; L'Amour has it lowered one sunny morning. LaBarge is aided in San Francisco by Capt. Hutchins, and his first mate aboard his schooner is Barney Kohl. The real-life firm of Hutchinson, Kohl & Company profited by buying Russian goods at the time of the Alaskan transfer. The manager of a commercial firm outside San Francisco in 1836–41 was named Alexander Rotchev and sent produce to Russian Alaska. *See* James R. Gibson, *Imperial Russia in Frontier America: The Changing Geography of Supply of Russian America, 1784–1867* (New York: Oxford University Press, 1976), 118, 127, 129, 132, 188, 245. This book is more recent than *Sitka*, but L'Amour undoubtedly consulted some of the same sources that Gibson used.

13. *See* Eugene Cunningham, *Triggernometry: A Gallery of Gunfighters* (New York: Press of the Pioneers, 1941; reprint, Caldwell, Idaho: Caxton Printers, 1982), 12, 34; Ed Bartholomew, *Bill Longley: A Texas Hardcase* (Houston: Frontier Press, 1953); and Bartholomew, *Cullen Baker: Premier Texas Gunfighter* (Houston: Frontier Press, 1954), which has valuable data and reprints Thomas Orr's 1870 *Life of the Notorious Desperado Cullen Baker, from His Childhood to His Death, with a Full Account of All the Murders He Committed.*

Chapter 4

1. In *Companion*, 98, L'Amour gives the time period of *The Daybreakers* as ca. 1870–72, but this handbook is inaccurate here (and elsewhere).

2. L'Amour was outraged by criticism of *Shalako* for having an improbable cast of characters; *see* his rejoinder, "An Open Letter to the Old Buckaroos," *Roundup* 11 (September–October 1963):2, 4–5.

3. Did L'Amour name these obscure classical military authorities to parade his love of the esoteric? He also mentions Vegetius in *The Daybreakers, The Walking Drum,* and *Education of a Wandering Man.*

4. *Kilrone* (New York: Bantam, 1966), 152; hereafter cited in text as *Kilrone*.

5. L'Amour agrees about this fine heroine. While commenting about the many "strong women" in his fiction, he notes that "I must admit that one of my favorites is Miss Jessica Trescott, of MATAGORDA. She was a lady of style, in everything she did" (*Companion*, 20, 21). For information on the checkered history of Matagorda Island, see Lyndal Waldrip, "Isle of Contention," *Texas Parks & Wildlife* 49 (November 1991):28–33.

6. *Down the Long Hills* (New York: Bantam, 1968), 44; hereafter cited in text as *Long Hills*.

7. This slip was noted in John D. Nesbitt, "Literary Convention in the Classic Western Novel," Ph.D. dissertation, University of California at Davis, 1980, 189n14; hereafter cited in text as Nesbitt, "Literary Convention."

Chapter 5

1. Don Walker, in "The Scholar as Mountain Man," *Possible Sack* 4 (April 1973):17, rebukes L'Amour for making Ronan Chantry a European-educated scholar "with . . . a headful of platitudes. This reference is hereafter cited in text as Walker, "Scholar."

2. "Nobody ever lived who was a finer judge of horseflesh than those Irish traders" (*The Sky-Liners* [New York: Bantam, 1967], 11; hereafter cited in text as *Sky-Liners*).

3. *The Man from Skibbereen* (New York: Bantam, 1973), 159; hereafter cited in text as *Skibbereen*.

4. *The Quick and the Dead* (New York: Bantam, 1973), 71, 80, 90, 93, 145, 164; hereafter cited in text as *Quick*.

5. *Rivers West* (New York: Bantam, 1975), 37; hereafter cited in text as *Rivers*.

6. The region called the Broken Hills is mentioned in "The Sixth Shotgun," reprinted in *The Outlaws of Mesquite*.

7. In a review of *Fair Blows the Wind*, in *Western American Literature* 13 (Winter 1979):365–66, William A. Bloodworth praises the novel for combining action and historical details, criticizes it for having too much coincidence, and chides L'Amour for attempting to replace western cowboys with European sword fighters.

8. This praise is well justified despite the criticism of *Bendigo Shafter* by Estleman, 44, for its alleged "stultifying aimlessness."

9. L'Amour, who relished the works of Poe all his life, reports that the hero of "Riding for the Brand," reprinted in the collection *Riding for the Brand*, borrowed books from Poe in Philadelphia and that the hero of *The Lonesome Gods* met Poe in the same city.

10. In a review of *Bendigo Shafter* and *Comstock Lode*, in *Western American*

Literature 16 (Winter 1982):315–17, John D. Nesbitt notes an autobiographical touch in the two novels: "Like Bendigo Shafter and L'Amour himself,
Trevallion marries an actress. Grita Redaway, as she has earlier told the villain,
will leave the theater only for the right man" (316). (L'Amour's wife also
abondoned an acting career, with no regrets.) Most of Nesbitt's review is
negative. *See also* his parody of L'Amour entitled "Adventures of the Ramrod
Rider, Price Ten Cents," *Colorado State Review* n.s. 11 (Spring–Summer
1984):56–59.

11. The open-endedness of the last chapter of *The Cherokee Trail* must
have encouraged many readers to hope that L'Amour would write a sequel. In
a 1982 interview, L'Amour hinted that Mary Breyton's Virginia plantation,
which would "be valuable again" after "a long time," might attract Mary
Breyton to return home one day (*The Lonesome Gods* [New York: Bantam,
1983], 460; hereafter cited in text as *Gods*).

12. L'Amour seemed to agree; see *The Shadow Riders* (New York: Bantam, 1982), 188–89; hereafter cited in text as *Shadow*.

Chapter 6

1. L'Amour liked the name Nesselrode. Nesselrode Clay is the name
of the Cactus Kid in "The Cactus Kid Pays a Debt," reprinted in *Long Ride
Home*, and "Love and the Cactus Kid," reprinted in *The Outlaws of Mesquite*.

2. This use of the refrain anticipates L'Amour's refrains in *The Walking
Drum*—"Your wit is a sword" and "*Yol bolsun*" (May there be a road). *Education*
also ends with the latter (234).

3. *Son of a Wanted Man* (New York: Bantam, 1984), 31; hereafter cited
in text as *Son*. The novel also has a time error. In *The Daybreakers,* the action
of which starts in 1866, Joe Sackett is 15. In *Borden Chantry* he is murdered
at about age 30, hence ca. 1881. The reader is told that the action in *Son*
occurs a few years later, or ca. 1885; but then the reader is informed that both
Jesse James (1847–82) and Billy the Kid (1859–81) are still alive.

4. The final climax is awkward, offstage, and narrated at secondhand.
One can almost hear L'Amour apologetically explaining that he knows such a
device is ridiculous but that he lacks time and interest to rewrite the ending.

5. L'Amour goes out of his way to criticize twelfth-century Christian
Europe for being intellectually stultified, theologically hidebound, and physically unsanitary.

6. The helpful endpaper maps are the best in any L'Amour book until
Last of the Breed and *The Sackett Companion*. L'Amour once informed an interviewer that before he wrote about a wandering character, "I get a big piece of
paper and I lay out the point of origin and the destination. Then I fill in all
along the route the character's going to travel" (Garry Abrams, "Louis
L'Amour Broadens His Frontiers," *Los Angeles Times*, 30 May 1984, V, 2).

7. For background on Sinan, *see* Marshall G. S. Hodgson, *The Order of Assassins* ('s-Gravenshage: Mouton & Co., 1955), 185–99; Bernard Lewis, *The Assassins: A Radical Sect in Islam* (New York: Basic Books, 1968), 110–18; and Enno Franzius, *History of the Order of Assassins* (New York: Funk & Wagnalls, 1969), 107–113.

8. L'Amour once stated that his personal library contained 20 books on costume (Keith, 24:9). See also *Education*, 199.

9. *The Walking Drum* (New York: Bantam, 1985), 281; hereafter cited in text as *Drum*.

10. *Passin' Through* (New York: Bantam, 1985), 182, 185; hereafter cited in text as *Passin'*.

11. In a review of *Last of the Breed*, in *Western American Literature* 23 (Spring 1988):84–85, Starr Jenkins complains that "the hero . . . seems to learn nothing from all his suffering. If anything, he regresses to a lower, more savage level of understanding, which is perhaps L'Amour's basic point about tribal-warrior life. Or any kind of warrior life" (84).

12. For contrasting comments on Lake Baikal, *see* "Buryatia: A Republic on Lake Baikal," *Soviet Life*, March 1988, 41–47, and Andrei Sakharov, *Memoirs* (New York: Alfred A. Knopf, 1990), 277–80. Since his death, L'Amour's suggestion has taken on the contours of a prophecy. *See* Nancy Shute, "From Unalaska to Petropavlovsk: Warm Welcomes Amid Geysers and Snow," *Smithsonian*, August 1991, 30–39, about well-heeled American tourists in Kamchatka and environs.

13. *Last of the Breed* (New York: Bantam, 1987), 32, 344; hereafter cited in text as *Breed*.

14. Fred Plog, "Prehistory. Western Anasazi," in *Handbook of North American Indians: Southwest*, vol. 9, ed. Alfonso Ortiz (Washington: Smithsonian Institution, 1979), 129.

15. Tony Hillerman, *Book World* 17 (14 June 1987):13. The definition of *sipapus* is from Hillerman. In *The Haunted Mesa*, L'Amour uses both numerical terms.

16. This attack was rehearsed in L'Amour's early story "Tailwind to Tibet," reprinted in *Night over the Solomons*.

17. A reviewer of *The Haunted Mesa* complains that "L'Amour's didactic approach and his needless repetition of details get in the way" (*Booklist* 83 [15 May 1987]:1386).

18. According to many obituary notices, L'Amour was proofreading *Education of a Wandering Man* only hours before he died.

19. A reviewer says "so banal is this memoir that one wonders if the late author regarded it as complete, or as the first draft it reads like," deplores its "pedestrian observations and homilies," and calls "L'Amour . . . surprisingly superficial in his own yarn" (*Publishers Weekly* 236 [1 September 1989]:73).

Chapter 7

1. In *Education* (98, 221, 248, 254, 257), L'Amour mentions Balzac, Cooper, and Faulkner, but never so as to indicate any artistic influence upon him.

2. Dianna Festa-McCormick, *Honoré de Balzac* (Boston: Twayne Publishers, 1979), 155; hereafter cited in text as Festa-McCormick. *See also* Mary Susan McCarthy, *Balzac and His Reader: A Study of the Creation of La Comédie Humaine* (Columbia and London: University of Missouri Press, 1982), 93, 94, 97–100.

3. *The Sackett Brand* (New York: Bantam, 1965), 13; hereafter cited in text as *Brand*.

4. Anthony Trollope, *An Autobiography* (Edinburgh and London: William Blackwood & Sons, 1883; reprint, London: Oxford University Press, 1950), 271–73; Winifred Gregory Gerould and James Thayer Gerould, *A Guide to Trollope* (Princeton: Princeton University Press, 1948), 183–84, 187–88, and elsewhere. From 1955, Bantam in "About the Author" blurbs began to quote L'Amour thus: "I could sit in the middle of Sunset Boulevard and write with my typewriter on my knees; temperamental I am not" (*Guns,* 149). Reese Hawkins wrote me (5 July 1984) that he once saw L'Amour typing an essay at his Caliente ranch while members of his family and their guests were playing cards in the same room.

5. Ada Galsworthy, preface to *The Forsyte Saga,* by John Galsworthy (New York: Charles Scribner's Sons, n.d.), vii; Festa-McCormick, 155; F. W. J. Hemmings, *The Life and Times of Emile Zola* (New York: Charles Scribner's Sons, 1977), 69.

6. *Comstock Lode* (New York: 1981), 421; hereafter cited in text as *Comstock.*

7. *Milo Talon* (New York: Bantam, 1981), 206; hereafter cited in text as *Milo.*

8. *Treasure Mountain* (New York: Bantam, 1972), 118; hereafter cited in text as *Treasure.*

9. *Jubal Sackett* (New York: Bantam, 1986), 306; hereafter cited in text as *Jubal.*

10. L'Amour cautioned his fans not "to put together a family tree of the Sacketts" because "I have not supplied all the names and relationships"; then he added, "there is no need now to list the names of the intervening generations, which will be done in due time" (*Companion,* 20, 256). Three generations separate Boyne and Shandy Sackett, four separate Malaby and Daubeny Sackett, and seven separate Philip and Parmalee Sackett. If the family tree in *The Sackett Companion* is any demographic guide, those multigenerational gaps might ultimately have been populated by one to two hundred additional Sacketts.

11. *Sackett's Land* (New York: Bantam, 1975), 29, 76, 136; hereafter cited in text as *Sackett's Land*.

12. One of L'Amour's most awkward time lapses occurs between chapters 29 and 30 of this novel. The action jumps from 1602, with Barnabas's children all young, to 1620, with the oldest sons mature and ready for independent adventures themselves.

13. *Lonely on the Mountain* (New York: Bantam, 1980), 14; hereafter cited in text as *Lonely Mountain*.

14. *Mojave Crossing* (New York: Bantam, 1964), 3–4; hereafter cited in text as *Mojave*.

15. *Mustang Man* (New York: 1966), 35; hereafter cited in text as *Mustang*.

16. *Galloway* (New York: Bantam, 1970), 149; hereafter cited in text as *Galloway*.

17. *The Man from the Broken Hills* (New York: Bantam, 1975), 133; hereafter cited in text as *Broken Hills*. L'Amour misidentified Emily Sackett Talon once as Emily Talon Sackett (*Gods,* 465). Strictly speaking, only Flagan and Galloway, who are brothers, and Tell are cousins; and Parmalee is by no means Tell's "second cousin," since their related forebears are brothers Malaby and Philip Sackett, eight generations back. But in the violent west, a well-armed "cousin" was a cousin was a cousin.

18. *Ride the River* (New York: Bantam, 1983), 183; hereafter cited in text as *Ride River*.

19. *Ride the Dark Trail* (New York: Bantam, 1972), 24; hereafter cited in text as *Ride Trail*.

20. *The Lonely Men* (New York: Bantam, 1969), 122; hereafter cited in text as *Lonely Men*. In *Frontier* (New York: Bantam, 1984), 66 (hereafter cited in text as *Frontier*), L'Amour points out that Col. Dearborn was "a distant relative of mine."

21. L'Amour, who found Riel fascinating, promised in the "Author's Note" preceding the text to write a novel about the man and "some other aspects of Western Canadian history." The work was evidently never written.

22. *The Daybreakers* (New York: Bantam, 1960), 3; hereafter cited in text as *Daybreakers*.

23. For verification, *see* Odie B. Faulk, *Dodge City: The Most Western Town of All* (New York: Oxford University Press, 1977), 157–63.

24. *Fair Blows the Wind* (New York: Bantam, 1978), 51; hereafter cited in text as *Fair Wind*.

25. Owen mentions that his "great-grandfather" escaped from Ireland to England and was advised to change his name (*Over on the Dry Side* [New York: Bantam, 1976], 23; hereafter cited in text as *Dry Side*). His new name was obviously Tatton Chantry. But wasn't that about three hundred years ago?

By his "great-grandfather," Owen must have meant something like his "great-grandfather's great-grandfather."

Chapter 8

1. *Tucker* (New York: Bantam, 1971), 15; hereafter cited in text as *Tucker*.

2. "How the West Was: A Conversation with Louis L'Amour," *Frontmatter: Book News from G. K. Hall & Co.* 2 (April 1980):2.

3. *The Ferguson Rifle* (New York: Bantam, 1973), 98; hereafter cited in text as *Ferguson*.

4. *The Proving Trail* (New York: Bantam 1979), 133; hereafter cited in text as *Proving*.

5. *The Mountain Valley War* (New York: Bantam, 1978), 10, 87; hereafter cited in text as *Valley War*.

6. Clarence Peterson, "L'Amour Detour: Western Writer Turns to the East," *Chicago Tribune*, 5 June 1984, 5, 2.

7. James Alexander Thom, review of *Jubal Sackett*, *Book World* 15 (16 June 1985):14; hereafter cited in text as *Thom*.

8. Reprinted in *Dutchman's Flat* (New York: Bantam, 1986), 158.

9. Reprinted in *Long Ride Home* (New York: Bantam, 1989), 110; hereafter cited in text as *Long Ride*.

10. *Radigan* (New York: Bantam, 1958), 144.

11. "A Ranger Rides to Town," reprinted in *Bowdrie's Law* (New York: Bantam, 1984), 127. L'Amour especially downplays his heroes' cursing. Thus, "Hopalong [Cassidy] . . . swore softly" (*Rustlers,* 127).

12. *The Iron Marshal* (New York: Bantam, 1979), 1; hereafter cited in text as *Marshal*.

13. *The Broken Gun* (New York: Bantam, 1966), 1; hereafter cited in text as *Broken Gun*.

14. *To Tame a Land* (New York: Bantam, 1984), 1; hereafter cited in text as *Tame Land*.

15. *Borden Chantry* (New York: Bantam, 1977), 14.

16. *The Rider of Lost Creek* (New York: Bantam, 1976), 123; hereafter cited in text as *Lost Creek*.

17. "The West of the Story," *Writer's Digest* 60 (December 1980):28.

18. Nesbitt, in "Literary Convention," 192, ridicules L'Amour for such violations of "aesthetic integrity."

19. *The Man Called Noon* (New York: Bantam, 1970), 37; hereafter cited in text as *Noon*.

20. *Bendigo Shafter* (New York: Bantam, 1979), 89; hereafter cited in text as *Bendigo*.

21. *To the Far Blue Mountains* (New York: Bantam, 1977), 92; hereafter cited in text as *Blue Mountains*.

22. *The High Graders* (New York: Bantam, 1965), 25. In his review of *Jubal Sackett,* Thom satirizes the overuse of this singsong rhythm when he writes: "Quaint is the prose that issues from Jubal Sackett . . . Stark and black are the tall trees . . . Long sits Jubal by the fire" (Thom, 14).

23. *Chancy* (New York: Bantam, 1968), 52; hereafter cited in text as *Chancy.*

24. *Hanging Woman Creek* (New York: 1964), 71.

25. *Silver Canyon* (New York: Bantam, 1957), 6; hereafter cited in text as *Canyon.*

26. Two other weaknesses in L'Amour's writings undermine his attempts at verisimilitude. The first weakness is his tin-ear use of diction which is inappropriately modern for fiction cast in the nineteen-century west. Here are a few examples, which could easily be quadrupled in number: "couldn't care less," "a fun time," "he is into piracy," "hopefully," "I have a thing about that," "long gone," and "we lucked out." The second weakness is L'Amour's occasional use of vague description. Here are two examples among many more. He writes that a certain girl "was dressed as any American girl of the period would be" (*Kilrone,* 47) and that a certain house "was more like an eastern house than a western house at this period" (*Noon,* 78). Why not put the reader back into the setting by direct depiction? Apropos of the unintegrated, *see* Don D. Walker on L'Amour's inartistic handling of source material for *Catlow,* in "Notes on the Popular Western," *Possible Sack* 3 (November 1971): 11–13.

27. Probably the first critic to note L'Amour's compositional errors was John D. Nesbitt, who in his review of *Bendigo Shafter* and *Comstock Lode* comments that "in these novels, as in all of L'Amour's fiction, there is a sprinkling of errors in grammar, sentence structure, and word usage" (*Western American Literature* 16 [Winter 1982]:315).

28. *Matagorda* (New York: Bantam, 1967), 119.

29. Walker capitalizes on one of L'Amour's seven hundred or so danglers, for humor: "At another point, as our hero [in *The Ferguson Rifle*] stalks the villains, the story breaks suddenly into violent action. 'Without thinking, my Ferguson came to my shoulder and I fired. One man stumbled, then fell.' In a novel in which the thinking is so shallow and fatuous, it is good to have a rifle that goes into action without even bothering to think" (Walker, "Scholar," 17).

30. *Brionne* (New York: Bantam, 1968), 104; hereafter cited in text as *Brionne.*

31. Author's note to "Four-Card Draw," in *Riding for the Brand* (New York: Bantam, 1986), 32.

32. "Showdown on the Tumbling T," reprinted in *The Outlaws of Mesquite,* 145. On aesthetic rather than grammatical grounds, Estleman objects when L'Amour in *Comstock Lode* permits "a backwoodsman to use 'ain't' and 'to whom' in the same sentence" (44).

Chapter 9

1. In *Education,* L'Amour praises Blackstone and Plutarch. He says that the former "was the key to much western law and in some areas the only law book known." He says of the latter, "I believe more great men have read his *Lives* than any other book, except possibly the Bible. . . . His is a sophisticated, urbane mind dealing with aspects of leadership" (188, 116, 117). L'Amour was proud of encouraging people to read certain authors, especially Plutarch, through having mentioned them in his novels. L'Amour wrote a Jamestown librarian once as follows: "I would venture to guess judging from my mail, that several hundred people, perhaps as many thousand, have read Plutarch because I spoke of him in my books" (quoted in Hawkins, 14). But L'Amour makes nothing whatever of the possibilities of contrasting pairs of heroic lives or pairs of men coming from different places or times, as Plutarch does. L'Amour does resemble Plutarch in minimizing history and stressing ethics.

2. Would Ruth Macken have been astute enough to buy and treasure a copy of *Walden* (1854) before the year 1860? It sold wretchedly up to that date and for several years thereafter. Furthermore, *Walden* is an inappropriate book to recommend to Bendigo, who properly encourages majority rule and then becomes town marshal.

3. *Reilly's Luck* (New York: Bantam, 1970), 159. For more of L'Amour's cowboys' reading lists, see *Chancy,* 65; *Proving,* 156–57; and *The Warrior's Path* (New York: Bantam, 1980), 29 (hereafter cited in text as *Warrior*).

4. The reader is referred to Klaschus, who discusses in depth L'Amour's knowledge of general history and real-life westerners, anti-academic bias, and historical naïveté; his opinions on Indians and theory of migration; his respect for the land and for natural beauty, topography, ecology, western occupations, and survival techniques; L'Amour and the Code of the West, western virtues, self-reliance, anti-racism, western etiquette, moderation, loneliness, goal orientation, pride, vigilantism, and aging; and his attitudes regarding women's liberation, sex, marriage, and family solidarity.

5. Evelyn G. Callaway, *Library Journal* 109 (1 November 1984):2064; anon., *Book World* 14 (2 December 1984):18.

6. L'Amour includes an awkward footnote reporting that the location is now the Mesa Verde National Park (*Dry Side,* 51). See also *Frontier,* 159–62.

7. L'Amour's fullest account of Escalante, also mentioned in *Galloway, Treasure Mountain,* and *Over on the Dry Side,* is in *Companion,* 178–79. L'Amour names a town Escalante in "Love and the Cactus Kid" (in *Outlaws*).

8. In *The Sackett Companion,* L'Amour discusses only the following historical figures named just above: Cullen Baker (121), Billy the Kid (230),

Wyatt Earp (238–39), Silvestre Escalante (178–79), Bat Masterson (238), and David Thompson (174).

9. Gary Topping, "Zane Grey's West," 39, in *The Popular Western,* ed. Richard W. Etulain and Michael T. Marsden (Bowling Green, Ohio: Bowling Green University Press, 1974).

10. *The Cherokee Trail* (New York: Bantam, 1982), 34; hereafter cited in text as *Cherokee.*

11. *High Lonesome* (New York: Bantam, 1962), 83–84.

12. *Kid Rodelo* (New York: Bantam, 1966), 62–63.

13. *See* Janet Faye Whiteaker, "Women Characters in Selected Novels of Louis L'Amour," M.A. thesis, Tennessee Technological University, 1981, and *Trail of Memories,* 33–43.

14. *How the West Was Won* (New York: Bantam, 1963), 83.

15. *Catlow* (New York: Bantam, 1963), 46.

16. *The Tall Stranger* (New York: Bantam, 1986), 88.

17. *Flint* (New York: Bantam, 1960), 98.

18. See author's note before "That Packsaddle Affair" (*Outlaws,* [115]).

19. Feminists may regard it as significant that this sweet-appearing "housewife" turns out to be a triple-dyed villainess.

20. *Hondo* (New York: Bantam, 1983), 59; hereafter cited in text as *Hondo.*

21. *The First Fast Draw* (New York: Bantam, 1959), 11.

22. *Under the Sweetwater Rim* (New York, 1971), 92.

Selected Bibliography

PRIMARY SOURCES

All publications, unless otherwise specified, are by Bantam Books. All paperback reprints, indicated by second dates, are by Bantam. A few novels had different earlier titles.

Novels

Bendigo Shafter. New York: E. P. Dutton, 1979 (hardcover); 1979.
Borden Chantry. 1977.
Brionne. 1968.
The Broken Gun. 1966.
The Burning Hills. New York: Jason Press, 1956; 1956.
The Californios. New York: Saturday Review Press, 1974 (hardcover); 1974.
Callaghen. 1972.
Catlow. 1963.
Chancy. 1968.
The Cherokee Trail. 1982.
Comstock Lode. 1981.
Conagher. 1969.
Crossfire Trail. New York: Ace, 1954; 1983.
Dark Canyon. 1963.
The Daybreakers. 1960.
Down the Long Hills. 1968.
The Empty Land. 1969.
Fair Blows the Wind. New York: E. P. Dutton, 1978 (hardcover); 1978.
Fallon. 1963.
The Ferguson Rifle. 1973.
The First Fast Draw. 1959.
Flint. 1960.
Galloway. 1970.
Guns of the Timberlands. New York: Jason Press, 1955; 1955.
Hanging Woman Creek. 1964.
The Haunted Mesa. 1987; 1988.
Heller with a Gun. Greenwich, Conn.: Fawcett, 1955; 1984.
The High Graders. 1965.

High Lonesome. 1962.

Hondo. Greenwich, Conn.: Fawcett, 1953; 1983.

Hopalong Cassidy and the Riders of High Rock (as Tex Burns). New York: Doubleday, 1951.

Hopalong Cassidy and the Rustlers of West Fork (as Tex Burns). New York: Doubleday, 1951; 1991 (hardcover, as by Louis L'Amour).

Hopalong Cassidy and the Trail to Seven Pines (as Tex Burns). New York: Doubleday, 1952.

Hopalong Cassidy, Trouble Shooter (as Tex Burns). New York: Doubleday, 1953.

How the West Was Won. 1963.

The Iron Marshal. 1979.

Jubal Sackett. 1985; 1986.

The Key-Lock Man. 1965.

Kid Rodelo. 1966.

Kilkenny. New York: Ace, 1954; 1983.

Killoe. 1962.

Kilrone. 1966.

Kiowa Trail. 1964.

Lando. 1962.

Last of the Breed. 1986; 1987.

Last Stand at Papago Wells. Greenwich, Conn.: Fawcett, 1957; 1986.

The Lonely Men. 1969.

Lonely on the Mountain. 1980.

The Lonesome Gods. 1983 (hardcover); 1983.

The Man Called Noon. 1970.

The Man from Skibbereen. 1973.

The Man from the Broken Hills. 1975.

Matagorda. 1967.

Milo Talon. 1981.

Mojave Crossing. 1964.

The Mountain Valley War. 1978.

Mustang Man. 1966.

North to the Rails. 1971.

Over on the Dry Side. New York: Saturday Review Press, 1975 (hardcover); 1976.

Passin' Through. 1985.

The Proving Trail. 1979.

The Quick and the Dead. 1973.

Radigan. 1958.

Reilly's Luck. 1970.

The Rider of Lost Creek. 1976.

Ride the Dark Trail. 1972.

Ride the River. 1983.

Rivers West. New York: Saturday Review Press, 1975 (hardcover); 1975.
Sackett. 1961.
The Sackett Brand. 1965.
Sackett's Land. New York: Saturday Review Press, 1974 (hardcover); 1975.
The Shadow Riders. 1982.
Shalako. 1962.
Showdown at Yellow Butte. New York: Ace, 1953; 1983.
Silver Canyon. New York: Avalon, 1956; 1957.
Sitka. New York: Appleton Century Crofts, 1957; 1958.
The Sky-Liners. 1967.
Son of a Wanted Man. 1984.
Taggart. 1959.
The Tall Stranger. Greenwich, Conn.: Fawcett, 1957; 1986.
To Tame a Land. Greenwich, Conn.: Fawcett, 1955; 1984.
To the Far Blue Mountains. New York: E. P. Dutton, 1976 (hardcover); 1978.
Treasure Mountain. 1972.
Tucker. 1971.
Under the Sweetwater Rim. 1971.
Utah Blaine. New York: Ace, 1954; 1984.
The Walking Drum. 1984 (hardcover); 1985.
The Warrior's Path. 1980.
Westward the Tide. London: World's Work, 1950; 1977.
Where the Long Grass Blows. 1976.

Short-Story Collections

Bowdrie. 1983.
Bowdrie's Law. 1984.
Buckskin Run. 1981.
Dutchman's Flat. 1986.
The Hills of Homicide. 1983.
Law of the Desert Born. 1983.
Long Ride Home. 1989.
Lonigan. 1988.
Night over the Solomons. 1986.
The Outlaws of Mesquite (hardcover). 1990.
The Rider of the Ruby Hills. 1986.
Riding for the Brand. 1986.
The Strong Shall Live. 1980.
The Trail to Crazy Man. 1986.
War Party. 1975.
West from Singapore. 1987.
Yondering. 1980.

Nonfiction

Education of a Wandering Man. Introduction by Daniel J. Boorstin. 1989 (hardcover); 1990.

Frontier. Photographs by David Muench. 1984 (hardcover).

The Sackett Companion: A Personal Guide to the Sackett Novels. 1988 (hardcover).

A Trail of Memories: The Quotations of Louis L'Amour. Compiled by Angelique L'Amour, foreword by Louis L'Amour. 1988 (hardcover).

Poetry Collection

Smoke from This Altar (hardcover). Oklahoma City: Lusk Publishing Co., 1939. Rev. ed., with introduction by Kathy L'Amour. New York: Bantam, 1990.

Miscellaneous Items

"Books in Their Saddlebags: The Men Who Made the Trail." *American West* 19 (July–August 1982):46–47, 68.

Forewords to *The Sackett Novels of Louis L'Amour.* 4 vols. Vol. 1, vii–ix. Vol. 2, vii–ix. Vol. 3, vii–viii. Vol. 4, vii–viii. 1980.

Letter to the editor, *Roundup* 26 (February 1988):27–28.

Letter to Wesley Laing, 14 September 1979. In *Kilkenny,* edited by Wesley Laing, xi. Boston: Gregg Press, 1980.

"A Letter to You from Louis L'Amour." *Waldenbooks: Booknotes,* April 1983, 1.

"Of Guns & Gunmen." *Gun World* 25 (September 1984):54–56.

"An Open Letter to the Old Buckaroos." *Roundup* 11 (September–October 1963):2, 4–5.

"The West of the Story." *Writer's Digest* 60 (December 1980):27–29.

"The West—The Greatest Story Ever Told." *Roundup* 29 (July–August 1981):4–7.

SECONDARY SOURCES

Bibliographies

Etulain, Richard W. "Louis L'Amour." In *A Bibliographical Guide to the Study of Western American Literature,* 181–82. Lincoln: University of Nebraska, 1982.

Gale, Robert L. "Louis L'Amour." In *Bibliography of American Fiction: 1919–1988,* edited by Matthew J. Bruccoli and Judith S. Baughman, vol. 1,

282–84. 2 vols., paged consecutively. New York and Oxford: Facts on File, 1991.

Hall, Hal W. *The Work of Louis L'Amour: An Annotated Bibliography & Guide.* San Bernardino, Calif.: Borgo Press, 1991. Includes both primary and secondary material.

Books

Bold, Christine. *Selling the West: Popular Western Fiction, 1860 to 1960.* Bloomington and Indianapolis: Indiana University Press, 1987. Places L'Amour in pop-culture tradition.

Century of Stories: Jamestown and Stutsman County. Compiled and edited by James Smorada and Lois Forrest. Jamestown, N. Dak.: Fort Seward Historical Society, 1983. Contains valuable material about Jamestown background of LaMoore family.

Crider, Bill. "Louis L'Amour." In *Dictionary of Literary Biography,* 240–45. New York: Scribner's, 1980. Detailed sketch.

Estleman, Loren D. *The Wister Trace: Classical Novels of the American Frontier.* Ottawa, Ill.: Jameson Books, 1987. Puts L'Amour in context.

Garfield, Brian. *Western Film: A Complete Guide.* New York: Rawson Associates, 1982. Contains data on movies made from L'Amour's fiction.

"L'Amour, Louis." In *Current Biography,* edited by Charles Moritz, 203–206. New York: H. W. Wilson Co., 1980. Includes discussion of L'Amour's ideas on writing and his historical accuracy.

Marsden, Michael T. "L'Amour, Louis (Dearborn)." In *Twentieth-Century Western Writers,* edited by James Vinson, 471–75. Detroit: Gale Research, 1982. Includes comments on L'Amour's geographical accuracy, use of family as theme, and depiction of women.

Marsden, Michael T. "Louis L'Amour." In *Fifty Western Writers: A Bio-Bibliographical Sourcebook,* edited by Fred Erisman and Richard W. Etulain, 257–67. Westport, Conn., and London: Greenwood Press, 1982. Includes discussion of L'Amour's major themes and survey of significant criticism of his works.

Phillips, Robert. *Louis L'Amour: His Life and Trails, An Unauthorized Biography.* Toronto and New York: PaperJacks Ltd., 1989; reprint *Louis L'Amour: His Life and Trails.* New York: Knightsbridge 1990. Derivative, hasty, careless, and unreliable.

Tuska, Jon, and Vicki Piekarski, eds. "Louis L'Amour." In *Encyclopedia of Frontier and Western Fiction,* 208–211. New York: McGraw-Hill Book Co., 1983. Biographical sketch.

Articles, Introductions, and Interviews

Abrams, Garry. "Louis L'Amour Broadens His Frontier." *Los Angeles Times*, 30 May 1984, pt. 5, 2. Interview.

Bannon, Barbara A. "Louis L'Amour." *Publishers Weekly* 204 (8 October 1973):56–57. Interview.

Barron, James. "Author Louis L'Amour Dies at 80; Chronicler of the American West." *New York Times*, 13 June 1988, D12. Obituary.

Bulow, Ernest L. "Still Tall in the Saddle: Louis L'Amour's Classic Western Hero." *Possible Sack* 3 (June–July 1972):1–8. On Characteristics of heroes in western fiction, including L'Amour's.

Evans, Jack. "Louis L'Amour: The Boy from North Dakota Who Made It Big . . . Biggest . . . in the Book Writing Business." *ND REC Magazine*, July 1981, 12–15. Personal reminiscence.

Gale, Robert L. "Louis L'Amour." In *Critical Survey of Long Fiction: Supplement*, 218–26. Pasadena: Salem Press, 1987. Surveys representative L'Amour novels.

Gonzalez, Arturo F., Jr. "Louis L'Amour: Writing High in the Bestseller Saddle." *Writer's Digest* 60 (December 1980):22–26. Useful biographical data.

Hawkins, Reese. "Louis L'Amour." *North Dakota Horizons* 5 (Spring 1975): 14–16. Personal reminiscence.

Hinds, Harold E., Jr. "Mexican and Mexican-American Images in the Western Novels of Louis L'Amour." *Latin American Literary Review* 5 (Spring–Summer 1977):129–41. Examines Mexican and Mexican-American characters in L'Amour's novels.

Hubbell, John G. "Louis L'Amour—Storyteller of the Wild West." *Reader's Digest* 117 (July 1980):93–98. Sprightly biographical essay.

Jackson, Donald Dale. "World's Fastest Literary Gun: Louis L'Amour." *Smithsonian* 18 (May 1987):154–56, 158, 160, 162, 164, 166, 170. Crisp account of L'Amour's methods and accomplishments.

Jarrod, Keith. Introduction to *Crossfire Trail*, by Louis L'Amour, v–x. Boston: Gregg Press, 1980. Valuable analysis.

Kalter, Suzy. "Louis L'Amour: He Tells How the West Was Really Won." *Family Weekly*, 10 June 1979, 4, 7. On L'Amour's writing habits and knowledge of history.

Keith, Harold. "Louis L'Amour: Man of the West." *Roundup* 23 (December 1975):1–2, 3, 12; 24 (January 1976):8–9, 11; 24 (February 1976):4–5. On L'Amour's early life, love of Oklahoma, and 1967 lecture at university there revealing writing techniques.

Laing, Wesley. Introduction to *Kilkenny*, by Louis L'Amour, v–x. Boston: Gregg Press, 1980. Valuable analysis.

Lee, Shirley. "Louis L'Amour and the Writers of the Purple Sage." *Collectibles Illustrated* 3 (January–February 1984):50–52. Features L'Amour's library.

Marsden, Michael T. "The Concept of the Family in the Fiction of Louis L'Amour." *North Dakota Quarterly* 46 (Summer 1978):12–21. On L'Amour and Indians, violence, family sagas, and concept of family.

Marsden, Michael T. "A Conversation with Louis L'Amour." *Journal of American Culture* 2 (Winter 1980):646–58. Relays L'Amour's self-promoting comments on family, career, popularity, audience, success, and work habits.

McDowell, Edwin. "Behind the Best Sellers." *New York Times Book Review,* 22 March 1981, 34. On L'Amour's reading background and popularity.

McMillan, Scott R. Introduction to *Showdown at Yellow Butte,* by Louis L'Amour, v–x. Boston: Gregg Press, 1980. Valuable analysis.

Nesbitt, John D. "Change of Purpose in the Novels of Louis L'Amour." *Western American Literature* 13 (Spring 1978):65–81. Reprinted in *Critical Essays on the Western American Novel,* edited by William T. Pilkington, 150–63. Boston: G. K. Hall, 1980. On change in L'Amour's fiction from formulary novels to family and historical novels.

Nesbitt, John D. "Louis L'Amour—Paper Mâché [*sic*] Homer?" *South Dakota Review* 19 (Autumn 1981):1–12. Criticizes L'Amour's post-1970 claims to being American frontier Homer and analyzes his simplistic treatment of character.

Nesbitt, John D. "Louis L'Amour's Pseudonymous Works." *Paperback Quarterly* 3 (January–April 1981):1–6. On L'Amour's "Tex Burns" and "Jim Mayo" writings.

Nuwer, Hank. "Louis L'Amour: Range Writer." *Country Gentleman* 130 (April 1979):99–100, 102. Contains extravagant praise.

Ring, Frances. "An Interview with Louis L'Amour." *American West* 19 (July–August 1982):48. On L'Amour's background and writing habits.

Sullivan, Tom. "Westward to Stasis with Louis L'Amour." *Southwest Review* 69 (Winter 1984):78–87. Suggests that L'Amour's heroes often fight for communities they then live in.

Tompkins, Walker A. "Meet Louis L'Amour." *Roundup* 2 (December 1954):3–4. Early biographical sketch.

Widener, Sandra. "The Untold Stories of Louis L'Amour: The West's Best-Selling Writer." *Post Empire Magazine* (Denver), 13 February 1983, 8–12, 14. On L'Amour's youth, years in Orient, army career, marriage and family, and plans.

Yagoda, Ben. "L'Amour Rides the Range." *Esquire* 91 (13 March 1979):22. Lively but general.

Index

The Author

Robert L. Gale received his B.A. from Dartmouth College and his M.A. and Ph.D. from Columbia University. He served in the U.S. Army Counter-Intelligence Corps in Europe during World War II and taught at Columbia, the University of Delaware, and the University of Mississippi, and in Italy and Finland on senior Fulbright fellowships. Until his retirement from the University of Pittsburgh in 1987, he taught courses there in American literature, Civil War literature, the American 1890s, the Roaring Twenties, and western American literature. He has written books on Henry James, Thomas Crawford, Nathaniel Hawthorne, Herman Melville, Edgar Allan Poe, and Mark Twain and is the author of the Western Writers Series booklets *Charles Warren Stoddard, Charles Marion Russell, Will Henry/Clay Fisher,* and *Matt Braun* and the Twayne's United States Author's Series volumes *Richard Henry Dana, Jr., Francis Parkman, John Hay, Luke Short,* and *Will Henry/Clay Fisher (Henry W. Allen).*

The Editor

Warren French (Ph.D., University of Texas, Austin) retired from Indiana University in 1986 and is now an honorary professor associated with the Board of American Studies at the University College of Swansea, Wales. In 1985 Ohio University awarded him a doctor of humane letters. He has contributed volumes to Twayne's United States Authors Series on Jack Kerouac, Frank Norris, John Steinbeck, and J. D. Salinger. His most recent publication for Twayne is *The San Francisco Poetry Renaissance, 1955–1960.*

Date Due

FEB 19 993			
APR 16 1993			
MAY -5 1993			
1/31 95	1:5257834		